KICK UP
SOME DUST

LESSONS

ON THINKING BIG,

GIVING BACK,

AND DOING IT

YOURSELF

KICK UP SOME DUST

BERNIE MARCUS

WITH CATHERINE LEWIS

WM

WILLIAM MORROW

An Imprint of HarperCollinsPublishers

HarperCollins books may be purchased for educational, business, or sales promotional use. For information, please email the Special Markets Department at SPsales@harpercollins.com.

FIRST EDITION

Photos courtesy of the authors

Library of Congress Cataloging-in-Publication Data has been applied for.

ISBN 978-0-06-325992-8

22 23 24 25 26   LSC   10 9 8 7 6 5 4 3 2 1

DEDICATED TO ALL THE HOME DEPOT
ASSOCIATES AND CUSTOMERS.
NONE OF THIS WOULD BE POSSIBLE WITHOUT YOU.

DEDICATED TO MY WIFE, BILLI,
WHO HAS BEEN SUCH A BIG PART OF THIS JOURNEY.

CONTENTS

CONTENTS

BREAKFAST WITH BERNIE

Frank Blake, former chairman and CEO
of the Home Depot

When I became CEO of Home Depot on January 3, 2007, replacing Bob Nardelli, the first call I made was to Bernie Marcus. Along with Arthur Blank and Ken Langone, he founded the retail icon, served as the first chairman and CEO, and led it for nineteen years through a period of explosive growth. Nobody knew more about Home Depot's business, culture, and values than Bernie. I knew it was important to talk with him. But I was not prepared for what followed.

Ken and I flew down to Boca Raton, Florida, to meet him for breakfast. It lasted four hours, long past the clearing of eggs, toast, and coffee. This was not a friendly, leisurely meal. It was like being in a blast furnace. Bernie was furious about what had happened to the company under Nardelli. He talked at length about what had gone wrong and was specific about what needed to be changed. He did all the talking. What poured out was the passion and love of a man for the business he founded, for the associates who worked there, and for the principles and values that made it unique. He would not tolerate those things being compromised in any way. This was personal, and I took it to heart. It was the most consequential breakfast of my career, and I kept my notes and drew upon Bernie's leadership lessons as I tried to fill his shoes.

I have a long list of what I call "Bernie-isms"—observations about human nature, business, generosity, and life. He once told me: "Frank, you have a prominent job at Home Depot, but not a significant one. Significant jobs are the ones serving customers. Never forget that." Another favorite: "When you go into a meeting at Home Depot and tell a joke, everyone will laugh. Just remember: You are not funny."

A few weeks after the Florida breakfast, I asked Bernie if he would speak at the Home Depot store managers' meeting in Dallas in March. This was the company's signature annual event, setting the tone for the whole year. It is attended by over three thousand leaders from around the country, from managers to merchants. I kept it a secret that Bernie was going to be there. I did the welcome and casually said, "Let me bring out the next speaker." When Bernie stepped out onto the stage, the crowd erupted in applause and cheers. To this day, it is the loudest, most heartfelt, and sustained cheering I have ever heard. It went on for more than five minutes. Grown men were crying. Truly. Full on tears. Bernie proceeded, without a script, to tell story after story. But what he really did was reconnect us all to what made Home Depot special.

He also did something else for me at that meeting, and the full weight of it would not hit me until later. When I took over as CEO, not many people outside of the top leadership at Home Depot knew me. My job was in business development, not in the day-to-day retail operations that are the core of the company. And I came to Home Depot after a decade at General Electric (GE). I was an unknown and an outsider. There was no reason for anyone to have any confidence in my selection. At that meeting, Bernie, literally and figuratively, put his arm around me. The thousands of HD leaders figured: "Well, if Bernie likes this guy, I guess we should give him a chance." How do I know this? Like all good companies, we polled the attendees afterward, and variations of that comment came up again and again. In all the years since that meeting, Bernie never once mentioned it to me. He never took credit for my success. He never said: "Frank, you owe me for that." He never expected anything in return—except that I lead the company with the values and integrity that made Home Depot so successful.

Henry Kissinger once said about Senator John Mc-Cain that "Heroes inspire us by the matter-of-factness of their sacrifice." Bernie inspires me by the matter-of-factness of his generosity. The managers' meeting story is one small example. There are so many others captured in this book. You will learn about Bernie's extraordinary efforts in building the largest aquarium in the world in 2005. Notice that he named it the Georgia Aquarium, not the Marcus Aquarium. Most visitors have no idea that Bernie gave the money to build it. I like to joke that if I were in a position to make such a gift, I'd call it "Frank's Fish." But Bernie needs no such recognition. He just wanted to thank the people who helped him build Home Depot.

This book is loaded with stories and anecdotes that show Bernie's impact on the lives of millions. Home Depot is only part of the story. He sees needs before others recognize them, as with autism, cancer research, and veterans' health. He finds opportunities where others are thwarted or frustrated. He has built things from scratch and changed the trajectory of struggling institutions, as he did with Grady Hospital.

There are people in this world who radiate energy and

people who absorb it. There are people who take their gifts and blessings and share them with others. And there are people who jealously guard what they have and keep their blessings to themselves. Bernie radiates energy and shares his gifts. He did that during our first breakfast, in the store managers' meeting, and in every interaction we've had since. He has taken what he helped build, multiplied it many times over, and shared it broadly and selflessly.

I have been fortunate to work for and learn from extraordinary leaders, including a Supreme Court justice (John Paul Stevens) and three U.S. presidents (Ronald Reagan, George H. W. Bush, and George W. Bush). I also love reading biographies about public figures, because you can glean so much from their experiences. But in the worlds of business and giving, there is no better source of inspiration than Bernie Marcus.

In reading this book, you will have the same opportunity that I had to learn from one of the world's most successful leaders. You get your own breakfast with Bernie. You can read it for the advice, the inspiring stories, and the humor. But you can also read it to get a sense of the animating passion underneath it all. We all want our work and lives to matter. In this book, Bernie gives you a blueprint to help make that happen. That is his gift to us both.

Frank Blake was the chairman and CEO of the Home Depot from January 2007 to May 2014. Prior to this, he held several executive roles at General Electric. He also served as general counsel for the U.S. Environmental Protection Agency, deputy counsel to Vice President George Bush, and law clerk to Justice John Paul Stevens of the U.S. Supreme Court. In 2017, he and Brad Shaw started the podcast "Crazy Good Turns."

WE CAN FACE
EVERYTHING AND RISE

Pitbull

After we met, Bernie asked me to come visit him at his house in Boca Raton. My crew and I drove up to the security gate, and they wouldn't let us in. I can't imagine why. I didn't have my identification, and I told them, respectfully, "I'm here to meet with Bernie Marcus." But they weren't buying it. No matter how many times Bernie called security, we weren't getting in. So, Bernie finally jumped in his car to come get me. When he arrived, the security team figured out that we weren't lying, but it seemed they just couldn't imagine a world where Pitbull and Bernie Marcus were friends.

On the surface, we couldn't be more different. He was a poor Jewish kid from Newark who became a pharmacist and hit it big with Home Depot in 1978. I'm a rapper and hustler who grew up in Miami in the 1980s around entrepreneurs selling a different kind of product. I learned English from watching *Sesame Street* and released my first album at the age of twenty-three. He's Bernie. I'm Mr. Worldwide. Take a closer look, and you'll see something else. We're like Warren Buffet and Jay-Z, Martha Stewart and Snoop Dogg. Our connection may not be obvious, but it's powerful.

We're both the children of immigrants. His parents fled Russia and Ukraine, and my grandmother resisted Fidel Castro. My aunt was a political prisoner. My mother was part of Operation Peter Pan in the early 1960s, and my father escaped Cuba and brought refugees over to America during the Mariel boatlift. Both of our families struggled to survive. Bernie's dad was a cabinetmaker, while his mother worked in a factory, like my grandmother. My father made sandwiches and hustled anything he could, and my mother cleaned houses and sold anything she could get her hands on.

Bernie and I both grew up on the streets—he joined a gang, and while I was never a troublemaker, I was always around trouble. We worked hard as kids—I parked cars at the Orange Bowl, cleaned birdcages, and worked at flea markets. Bernie cleaned toilets and worked at a bowling alley. But we had loving parents who believed in this country and risked everything for freedom and a slice of the American Dream.

Bernie and I first met in my hometown, in the Little Havana neighborhood of Miami. He came to see what we were doing at SLAM! (Sports Leadership Arts and Management Academy)—our first public charter school for students, kindergarten through high school. As a kid, I went to all kinds of different schools in all kinds of neighborhoods. Most were built to fail. But I learned that a great teacher or mentor can save your life. For me, it was Hope Martinez, who taught me in high school. She believed in me and gave me that boost I needed. I've always believed that life has a way of putting amazing people in our paths, so I invited Bernie to come to our school and tell his story. I'm sure the kids were thinking: Who is this old guy? What does he know about our lives? But then he started talking—and they started listening. He was funny, blunt, and not afraid to tell the truth. Kids love that. It all came down to one message: Work hard and challenge yourself. He didn't tell them what they wanted to hear, but what they needed to hear: Nobody is going to do it for you; you've got to do it yourself. I couldn't have said it better. We now have twelve SLAM! schools, and we're building more every year. We get to help this new generation stand up, make a difference, and change the world. I'm proud that Bernie got to see that firsthand, and I'm grateful for the wisdom he shared with those kids.

Another thing I love about Bernie is his generosity. People who make it big either sit around and count their money, or they get to work helping people. When my career took off, I realized that I could use my fame to make a difference in others' lives. I could have an endless string of number one records, but on their own they mean nothing. I could keep performing in front of the sold-out crowds around the world, but in the end, it has to mean something. Giving back to my community matters because it provides me the opportunity to build more, do more, give more. When you read this book, you'll see that Bernie does the same thing. He cares about education, free enterprise, medicine, and veterans. He cares about the community the same way I do.

Kids of immigrant parents know something that other kids don't: The biggest gift you have is your freedom. When I talk to people who are on the fence about the United States, I always say that I'm here to make sure we stay the United States, not the divided states. Freedom isn't perfect, but freedom is priceless. This country has problems, but when you see what's happening in other parts of the world, you understand how lucky you are and how much your parents sacrificed for you to grow up here in America. I know, and Bernie knows.

If you're an entrepreneur, you've got to be a bit of a hustler. Nothing should hold you back from your vision or your goals. If you focus and you believe, you can make anything happen. And when you do, you should reach out and help those who haven't had their chance yet. I like to say there is only one race—the human race. We all have the same blood. We all breathe the same air. We all deserve the same opportunity. My parents and Bernie's parents took the biggest chance of all, so I look in the mirror every day to ask if I'm making the most of the opportunities provided to me. Am I doing my best for myself and for others? Figure out how to answer that question, and you'll see that the harder you work, the more opportunities will come your way.

I'm glad you're reading this book. Bernie is a very special man with a very special vision, and we have a strong connection. We both figured out what the world needed at exactly the right time. Home Depot helped people build homes, neighborhoods, and communities. In his vision for it, he made it affordable. He made it easy. He made it possible for you to do it yourself. I did it with music across languages and cultures around the world. My first name, Armando, can be translated to mean "to build"—another point of connection between us. Music builds bridges and puts joy back into the world. That's where my inspiration for "I Believe That We Will Win" came from. With the right attitude, we can face everything and rise.

Bernie and I have talked a lot about what really matters—and how to make a difference. I tell him that my mother taught me that you shouldn't take "no" for an answer. I like when people say "you can't, you won't, you never will," because it lets us prove them wrong. Read this book, and you'll see that Bernie also believes that every "no" is just a new opportunity. In "can't" there is "can." In "don't" there is "do." And in "impossible" there is "possible." In Miami we'd say, *"Ponte las pilas, pa lante que no ay mas nada, pasos cortos y vista larga siempre,"* which translates roughly as "put your batteries in (and get going)" and "short steps, long vision," or as Bernie would say, "You gotta find the chutzpah to kick up some dust."

Armando Christan Pérez (Pitbull) has sold more than 25 million albums and over 100 million singles worldwide, and he has over 15 billion YouTube views. He has performed in over fifty countries for millions of people and is also a motivational speaker and global brand ambassador. In addition to his music and business endeavors, Pitbull focuses his philanthropy on education and the environment.

KICK UP
SOME DUST

CAPITALISM IS NOT A DIRTY WORD

The start of Home Depot sounds like the beginning of a bad joke: "Two Jews and an Italian decide to build a new kind of hardware store . . ." My father was a cabinetmaker, and my mother suffered from debilitating rheumatoid arthritis. There were four children in my family, and we never had any money. I graduated from Rutgers, worked for two different pharmacies and then a chain of discount stores called Two Guys, before taking the helm at Handy Dan Home Improvement, headquartered in Southern California. Who would have ever guessed that being fired by Sandy Sigoloff—Mr. Chapter 11—would be the best thing that ever happened to me? That is not what I was thinking on April 14, 1978.

Here I was, unemployed, just when most of my friends were looking forward to retirement. But I was not alone. My friends Arthur Blank, Handy Dan's chief financial officer, and Ron Brill, our comptroller, also found their heads on the chopping block. Long before that fateful day, I had been dreaming of transforming the home improvement business by creating a huge warehouse-style store that stocked everything you might need at low prices. Add great customer service to the mix, and I was sure this would be a winning formula. I briefly mentioned the details of my plan to Ken Langone, who would later organize the financing for Home Depot, a few years earlier, but didn't share any of the details. When I called Ken to tell him about being fired, he laughed and said, "Bernie, you just got kicked in the ass with a golden horseshoe." It took me awhile to see that he was right. Now I had the opportunity to start the new business that I had been imagining—to reach my very own American Dream. It was *beshert*—destiny—something that would happen again and again throughout my life. Sometimes things work out just the way they should, whether you want them to or not.

On opening day, June 22, 1979, our kids stood at the entrance giving out $1 bills to lure in shoppers. By dinner time they still had plenty of cash. We were devastated, and I remember that my wife would not let me shave the next day because she did not want a razor in my hands. But we were passionate about our idea, understood the risks, were not afraid of failure, and told our story to anyone who might help us meet our goal. These four factors helped us become the world's largest home-improvement retailer. At the heart of it all was the belief in the concept of do-it-yourself.

After Home Depot went public in 1981, I was playing golf with a friend, and he told me that we were going to go out of business. That was news to me, so I asked him to explain.

He said, "I came in to purchase a $200 faucet, but they told me that I needed a washer that cost less than two dollars. And the guy showed me how to fix it. So, you guys lost a big sale. If you keep doing that, you'll be bankrupt in no time."

Leaning on my sand wedge, I smiled. "Tell me this. Where would you go if you had a problem with your plumbing again?"

"Home Depot, of course," he answered.

We weren't geniuses, we just knew that people were hungry for help and needed the confidence, tools, and support to take on their own home improvement projects. This story illustrated our core values, and we trusted our associates to do right by the customer. That's how we transformed an industry and made it big.

YOU MIGHT SAY THAT "DO-IT-YOURSELF" HAS BEEN THE theme of my entire life. By the time I was fifteen, I had held more than a dozen jobs, joined a gang, worked as a comedian and hypnotist in the Catskills, and saw my mother, a survivor of the Triangle Shirtwaist Factory fire, scrape our pennies together to help people she would never meet. We had no safety net, and I learned early on that if I was going to survive, I could not wait for others to solve my problems. If I wanted to go to a baseball game, I had to find my own way to Yankee Stadium. If I wanted to make more money in tips, I had to come up with a good comedy routine. If I could not afford medical school, I had to pursue a different degree. If I wanted to break into retail in a big way while working at Two Guys early in my career, I had to figure out how to beat our competition at selling one of our most popular and profitable items—Revlon lipsticks. If I wanted to change the way hardware was sold in America, I had to think big.

The belief in do-it-yourself extended well beyond Home Depot into my giving. My wife, Billi, and I long ago promised to donate our money in our lifetimes, and we were early supporters of the Giving Pledge. When I co-founded Home Depot, we were broke. But I knew that I lived in a country where a simple idea—do it yourself— helped create a company that now employs nearly 500,000 people and has helped thousands of other companies succeed. I was given plenty of opportunity, and I feel a deep sense of debt and gratitude to those who made it possible.

I am proud of the thousands of Home Depot associates and millions of customers that have made it possible for the Marcus Foundation to donate more than $2 billion to charity. I feel a responsibility to them to put in the hard work to truly solve a problem and save lives. I'm sure that you have things that you care deeply about, problems you want to see fixed. Donating money is easy; getting involved and making a difference is hard. The same kind of energy that made you successful in your business can shape your giving. You have to put your heart and soul into what you care about, and "do it yourself." This book is not about me. I tell my story with the hope that it will help you see how your own effort, dedication, and sacrifice can bring hope and satisfaction in your life. All great causes need help, and if you have skills in marketing, law, public relations, sales, or any other field, you have a duty to get involved. Let me show you what I mean.

In 1988, Orthodox Jews in Israel sought to amend the Law of Return to restrict the definition of who is Jewish. The uproar around the world was fierce, especially in the United States, where less than ten percent of Jews identified as Orthodox. It was very personal for me because I had a daughter-in-law who converted to Judaism, meaning that my grandchildren would not be considered

Jewish if the new law passed. Leaders around Atlanta held a meeting at the Jewish Federation on Spring Street, and afterward I called Dr. Ken Stein, professor of contemporary Middle Eastern history at Emory University, for guidance. Ken explained how broken Israel's parliamentary system was and how much time they spent fighting internal squabbles, while existential battles raged all around them. The fight over this law was a symptom of a bigger problem.

I was no legal scholar, but I knew that the country needed help. Ken led me to Dr. Arye Carmon at the Israel Diaspora Institute at Tel Aviv University, who then introduced me to George Shultz, the outgoing secretary of state under Ronald Reagan. After a series of trips and meetings, I agreed to fund the formation of the Israel Democracy Institute (IDI) in 1991. The institute had a simple goal: to be an independent, non-partisan think tank supporting democratic principles. To do that, we hired lawyers, scholars, and graduate students to help members of the Israeli parliament—the Knesset—create a legislative infrastructure. We built a library and paid for staff to support committee members. George, who had long been engaged with Israel, created an advisory council that included U.S. Supreme Court Justice Stephen Breyer, Canadian Supreme Court Justice Rosalie Abella, and other legal giants.

The most important thing George did was suggest building a round table to ensure that nobody sat at the head. He then promised any politician that they could have private meetings with scholars and policy experts from around the world. In this way, they could hash out controversial issues without having to accommodate their constituents, the media, or worry about reelection. As the only democracy in the Middle East, Israel is essential to stability in the region and is one of our main strategic partners. Because of IDI, Israeli leaders now use research and data about laws and programs that have succeeded or failed in other democracies to enact legislation that serves the Israeli people, from the ultra-Orthodox to Arab-Israelis. The lesson? Don't be satisfied to solve little problems. Think big. Debate over one bad law led to the creation of Israel's premier policy research and advocacy organization and a global model worthy of emulation.

My second example involves people we all care deeply about: veterans. During a tour in 2007 of the Shepherd Center in Atlanta—a facility the Marcus Foundation had been supporting for years—I picked up a copy of the summer edition of their magazine, *The Spinal Column*, and saw a young Army soldier on the front cover. His name was Eric Jordan. At twenty-three, I learned, he had been injured in Iraq by an improvised explosive device (IED). After being treated at Walter Reed National

Military Medical Center in Washington, D.C., and later the James A. Haley Veterans' Hospital in Tampa, he was released and told that he would just "have to live with his injuries." It was as if this young man had been thrown out with the trash. The VA just gave up on him.

But Carrie, Eric's mother, did not. Through intensive research, she learned about the Shepherd Center's Beyond Therapy program. Drawing upon cutting-edge research, the intensive activity-based outpatient program helps people with spinal cord injuries maximize muscle and neural return, decrease complications, and promote lifelong health. But there was a big catch: It was expensive, and the Jordans could not afford it. Carrie started negotiating with the VA and Eric's doctors to see if he could qualify for the program, and after months of calls her persistence finally paid off. In January 2007, he started coming to Shepherd three times a week. After two days, Eric stood on a tilt table; after four weeks, he could walk. Tina Candelaria, the outpatient services coordinator for Beyond Therapy, was so inspired by Eric's journey that she started navigating the bureaucracy at the VA to see if she could help Jeffery Glasser, another soldier. When I saw the program's potential, I called Alana Shepherd, whose family founded the center, to ask, "Do you get a lot of veterans coming for treatment?"

She replied, "All the time, but we can't take them.

Most insurance will not cover it, and the VA is impossible to deal with. Sometimes they give veterans support, then it mysteriously disappears. The treatment can be tens of thousands of dollars, and most families don't have that kind of money."

I said, "Alana, let's do something about this." I was not a doctor, but I knew that these veterans needed help, and we needed to think big.

The Marcus Foundation gave a $2 million grant as seed funding, and Shepherd launched the SHARE (Shaping Hope and Recovery Excellence) Military Initiative in 2008 with the tagline "Hope is Here." That single magazine article helped change the trajectory of our community giving. We have devoted millions to veterans' causes, supported dozens of organizations, and recently partnered with Arthur Blank to together give $40 million to create the Avalon Network to treat post-traumatic stress disorder (PTSD) and traumatic brain injury (TBI), because no Americans deserve more support than the men and women who risk their lives to protect our nation. The lesson? True success requires help. The best solutions leverage the talent and energy of partners who share the same passion and goals.

What do these stories have in common? I do not believe there is a single, winning formula for success either in retail or giving. But you have to begin with the belief that you can "do it yourself." You don't have to have millions or even thousands of dollars to make a phone call and do research to try to solve a problem. And you don't have to do it alone. But you have to believe you have the ability to make a difference. I was no expert on Israeli law or traumatic brain injury, but I cared about each of these things deeply, was willing to ask questions, dig into the details, and then invest in a team of experts. That's what we did at Home Depot. If you see a problem at your school or job or in your neighborhood, stand up and do something. You can't just sit back and let others do the work—you have to kick up some dust. In the chapters that follow, I distill the lessons I have learned in my ninety plus years to show that when you "do it yourself," you can make a difference and maybe even change the world.

THESE DAYS, BUILDING A PROFITABLE BUSINESS IS RE-garded as something evil. It's like everybody believes that famous Balzac quote, the epigraph to *The Godfather*: "Behind every great fortune there is a crime." But I have nothing to apologize for. I am the son of immigrants who fled the violence of eastern Europe and came through Ellis Island in the early twentieth century with nothing. I grew up poor and made it the old-fashioned way: I had bold plans, took big risks, and helped build one of America's most iconic businesses. The companies I helped run and build have employed hundreds of thousands of people, paid billions in wages, launched and supported dozens of other companies, and contributed hundreds of billions to the U.S. gross domestic product. Home Depot created thousands of millionaires, many of whom never went to college. The products and services we sold helped millions of Americans by lowering hardware prices and made home building affordable across the country. That is the miracle of the free market.

Throughout this book, I will show you that the secrets we used to build and run a Fortune 500 company are the same ones that can help you tackle big problems, bring about change to your community, and be a positive force in the world. You don't have to wait until you are successful to give back, and when you retire, you should use the skills learned in your career to improve your community. Andrew Carnegie, the famous nineteenth-century industrialist, once said, "It is more difficult to give away money intelligently than to earn it in the first place." The same things that my mother taught me and that made Home Depot successful helped us establish the Marcus Foundation. How we did it and how you can, too, is at the heart of this book.

CHAPTER 1

GET SOME CHUTZPAH

A few years ago, a guy named Alex Katz came to my office to see if we would like to invest in the Cleveland Cord Blood Center's umbilical cord research. We had been interested in funding new therapeutics and had done a lot with stem cells, so I was happy to hear his pitch. As the conversation wound down, I asked Alex what he did for a living. Turned out that he and his brothers, Peter and David, ran a family business called Kason Industries in Newnan, Georgia, about half an hour south of Atlanta. The company started as a five and dime in Brooklyn back in 1926. After probing a little more, we realized that his grandfather, Abraham, made hinges for the commercial refrigerators that my father, Joseph, used to build and sell to grocery stores. I used to go to Brooklyn with my dad twice a year as a child to visit their factory and re-membered Alex's grandfather well. What are the chances? How did Jews whose fathers worked together in New York and New Jersey end up in the hardware business in Georgia talking about cutting-edge medical research? Everybody has a story, and you never know where you might find a point of connection. After he left, I sat down at my desk only to look up and see my father's carpentry tools framed on my wall. Boy, had we come a long way.

MY PARENTS IMMIGRATED TO AMERICA WITH NO money in the early twentieth century when they were children to escape the poverty and antisemitism in eastern Europe. My mother, Sara Schinofsky Marcus, was born in the Ukraine in 1896, and my father, Joseph Marcus, was born in Russia in 1889. They rarely discussed anything with their four children about their lives in Europe. We would occasionally catch an unfamiliar Russian word, and I remember that my mother once talked about the po-groms in her hometown. She used to say that Easter was the most dangerous time of the year, because the Cos-sacks, paramilitary units used by the Russians, would ride through the villages and terrorize the Jews, sometimes even cutting off men's heads. This was a past they wanted to shield us from.

I cannot imagine the courage it took to come here—they did not speak English, they made a dangerous journey halfway around the world, and they left a country that had been home to their family for generations. They met in Newark and lived in a fourth-floor walk-up tenement on Rose Street. I was born in 1929, the youngest of four children. I used to joke that they tore it down to build a slum.

My father was a cabinetmaker. He was strong as an ox, and a great craftsman, but a terrible businessman. You might think that his profession explained how I came to build Home Depot, but you'd be wrong. Most nights, my father came home, took a bath, poured a small glass of schnapps, and sat by the window while my mother fed the four of us. When we finished, we left the kitchen and they ate together. We only ate with them on Friday nights and the weekends. I knew almost nothing about what he did, and he never taught me any of his woodworking skills.

My most vivid memory of my father is the day that my mother caught me swinging from the fire escape on our building. She was hysterical. "Wait until your father gets home," she kept saying. This was unusual because my mother was the disciplinarian, so this scared me. I remember waiting anxiously by the front door for him and even putting a book in my pants for padding, worried about what was going to happen. I recall that he took me into the back room, looking as uncomfortable as I was scared, and said, "Bernie, I have to spank you. Your mother insisted, so we might as well get it over with. And promise me that you will not ever swing from the fire escapes again. You could be seriously hurt." He removed the book and hit me with a pot on my backside, and I was black and blue for a week. It is the only time he touched me, and it gave him no pleasure. He apologized profusely when he was finished; he kept saying over and over again in Yiddish—*ikh bin nebekhdik*—I am sorry.

Newark had a big Jewish population, about 50,000, mostly concentrated near Prince Street in the Old Third Ward. The streets were always teeming with Jews speaking Yiddish and bargaining with pushcart owners who sold everything from herring to pickles—it was like Orchard Street in the Lower East Side of New York. You could find kosher butchers and delis—Halper's Paper Goods, Bakalchuk the Tailor, Hupert's Fish Market. My father had his workshop there, and there were five synagogues on Prince Street and eleven more close by, the oldest being Congregation Adath Israel Mishnayes. We were raised in an Orthodox home, keeping kosher and staying active in our community. My father went to synagogue, and we went as a family on the holidays. At first, we lived about a mile from Prince Street, then we moved a little farther out and had to walk four miles to get to synagogue in all kinds of weather.

It was a close-knit community. One day, I remember seeing a public auction for who would be on the bimah (the podium in a synagogue from which the Torah is read) for the High Holy Days. This was a way to raise money for the synagogue, and the winner would be called to the bimah to recite a blessing before the reading of the Torah, what we call an Aliyah. On this one occasion, two rival Jewish gangs were in the congregation and started to bid against each other. They bid the honor up to $5,000—this at a time when the minimum wage was twenty-five cents and an average annual salary was $474. So, imagine a sum like that. I can still see the stunned faces of the people just sitting there.

These gang members were dangerous criminals, better known for murder, racketeering, and extortion. But they were also a source of protection for Jews, especially from the German American Bund. This antisemitic organization was made up of people of German ancestry who supported the Nazi Party in America. Formed in 1936, three years after Hitler came to power in Germany, the bund operated youth training camps and developed more than seventy divisions across the country. They are most famous for holding an "Americanization" rally at Madison Square Garden on February 20, 1939. The famous aviator Charles Lindbergh was a supporter of the bund and the America First Committee, the foremost isolationist group in the U.S. We saw the bund marching in Newark, Union City, and Griggstown with swastikas and Nazi salutes—a terrifying sight for any kid. But we also heard that the Jewish gangsters in New Jersey and New York—like the ones I saw in synagogue—beat up members of the bund on the streets with pipes and baseball bats. I always secretly hoped it was some of the guys that bid for the bimah.

A LITTLE DIPLOMACY

My mother, Sara, was a remarkable woman—the diplomat of the neighborhood. If there was an issue, people came to her for advice. She would have been a great rabbi because she had a way of always looking at the bright side of things. I remember when one of my uncles died, my mother said, this was a good thing. I did not understand until she explained, "He was in a lot of pain, and he has peace now and so does his family." She was optimistic about everything—never complained, never seemed upset or defeated. That is amazing considering what she experienced as a teenager.

My mother sewed garments at the Triangle Shirtwaist

Factory in Manhattan, a sweatshop in every sense of the word. The factory employed about six hundred immigrant women like my mother to work on sewing machines for twelve hours a day in terrible conditions for fifteen dollars a week. Located on the top three floors of the Asch Building, the factory had two stairwells that were locked from the outside and only one working elevator. On the afternoon of March 25, 1911, when my mother was fifteen years old, a fire broke out. The manager tried to use the fire hose to extinguish it, but the valve was rusted shut. Everyone panicked—some girls jumped down the elevator shaft or out the windows to their deaths, others were burned alive at the bottom of the locked stairwells. In eighteen minutes, 145 workers were killed. It was the deadliest industrial disaster in the history of the city. My mother survived. That might help explain where she got her strength and courage.

As a young wife and mother, she taught at several business schools until she was crippled by rheumatoid arthritis. Her hands and feet were like gnarled tree limbs. By the time she was in her mid-thirties, she was confined to her bed and in constant pain. She had recently had a miscarriage and was exhausted. My family was nearly destitute because my father only had occasional work. My three older siblings had to cook, clean, and do the laundry—I have no idea how they managed. It sounded like a pretty desperate situation. My sister, Beatrice (Bea), was about eight years old when a Jewish doctor came to the house to explain that the only way my mother might ever walk again was to have another baby. He gave her some hormone shots to help, and my parents decided to give it a try. I was born on Mother's Day in 1929, five months before the stock market crash that began the Great Depression. They called me the miracle baby because, indeed, after I was born, my mother got out of bed and started walking and caring for the house again.

AS POOR AS WE WERE DURING THE DEPRESSION, MY mother occasionally gave us snack money. This was a rare treat. Sometimes we'd buy what was called a Charlotte Russe. This fancy eighteenth-century European dessert, which cost a nickel, somehow made it to the streets of New York and New Jersey in the early twentieth century. The American version had a thin piece of sponge cake topped with whipped cream and a big, red cherry. They were sold from pushcarts, bakeries, and candy stores, though only in the spring or fall, because heat melted the cream. In hard times, they were a luxury that kept us kids going.

But there were days when my mother gave that snack money to charity. I used to complain, but she was unmoved. She firmly believed in the Jewish concept of tzedakah, which means simply "to give back." It is considered a mitzvah (good deed) to give to someone who has less than you have. She would put the coins in a *pushke*, a little metal box that we kept in our kitchen. In the 1930s, it probably did not amount to much, maybe a few dollars a year. She might give it to a needy neighbor or send it to Israel to plant trees. When she tried to explain her reasons to me, I was mad at first and wouldn't listen. But the lesson started to sink in. Soon I was asking: "Who are we giving the money to this week?" Instead of pouting, I had become a participant. She showed me how much charity mattered, and in the process, taught me something that has shaped my entire life.

We first lived at 86 Rose Street across from Fisher's Bakery in a mixed neighborhood—Jewish, African American, Polish, Italian. I had red hair, freckles, and blue eyes so I didn't look like I belonged to *any* group. There were about a hundred children in my building, which was paradise for a kid. But we did not have much—if my father did not bring home money we did not eat. In those days, you had no safety net—there were no food stamps when you could not feed your children, no social security when you retired, or unemployment if you lost your job. My father's brother, Daniel Marcus, had some money, but he never helped us. His other siblings lived close by, so we regularly walked to one another's houses. We were clearly the poorest of the bunch. A few times a year, we had a big family meeting in the basement of one of the social halls. Everybody brought food, and we talked about the issues of the day. I rarely saw them once I was in college, and, eventually, our family lost contact with most of the family.

My three siblings were much older than me. Irving, the eldest, was born in 1917. He was twelve when I came along, and I almost never saw him. He worked while going to college at Rutgers to study accounting and helped support the family. He was twenty-four when Pearl Harbor was attacked, and his entire class at Rutgers was drafted into the glider program in the Army. Here were all these nerdy accountants flying troops and heavy equipment into combat zones. One day, he was too sick to fly, so his friend Myron Needle took his place. The glider crashed, and Myron was killed. My brother was devastated, but he was determined to become a pilot anyway, and applied to flight school. When he was rejected, he ended up in the infantry in Europe and fought in the Battle of the Bulge, the last major German offensive on the Western Front. It was a brutal campaign, and years later Irving finally told us what had happened. They had inadequate ammunition, clothing, and food. They were bombed constantly, and he watched people being killed right in front of him. When he returned home, he exhibited all the symptoms of post-traumatic stress disorder—but back then, we did not know what that was. People just called it "shell shock." After the war, he became an accountant and always cared for my parents and our family, but he was never the same.

Seymour (Sy) was born in 1919 and was ten years older than me. He also served in the war but developed an ulcer and was discharged. He became a stockbroker and moved to Canada. Then there was Beatrice, who was born in 1923. She was eight years older than me and was more like a mother than a sibling. My mother was still struggling with her arthritis after I was born, so Bea took care of me. We shared a room until I was a teenager, and I loved her dearly. Bea protected me from my older brothers and often covered for me when I got into scrapes in the neighborhood. Anytime I had to get stitches, she would help me make up an excuse. When I think about my family, I mostly think about Bea, and we stayed close until the day she died. I am sure that my siblings resented, to some degree, having another mouth to feed, but I know they also always believed that my birth helped save our mother's life.

YOU WEARING ME OUT

Because I was so much younger, I was pretty much forgotten. From about the age of nine, I roamed the streets most days when I was not in school, and my parents often did not know where I was. I hung out with friends. I worked on my bicycle and a makeshift skateboard, both of which I had built from scraps I found around the neighborhood. Other times I ventured out alone. I met some people who worked for a circus. I loved to observe and study people and even thought I might become a psychiatrist. With all the costumes and makeup, the animals, games, and performances, the circus seemed like a glamorous place to start trying to figure out what made people tick. I loved the sideshows and helped clean up at night to earn a little extra money. While this did not last long, I do remember writing an English paper about the realities of circus life. It was here that I honed my observational skills and learned to trust my intuition; both would later become important in my career.

We moved to a larger apartment on Belmont Avenue in 1939 when I was about ten, and I went to a predominantly black middle school. I had a big mouth and was a bit of a class clown. What made me charming in elementary school made me a pain in the ass in middle school. I drew the attention of boys like Big Jim.

Big Jim was older than me and a lot bigger, and he beat me to a pulp nearly every day. I would show up the next day and fight him again. I was a tough kid who was not afraid to get into a fight, especially if somebody called me a "dirty Jew," which was a common put-down. After a few weeks of scrapes, Big Jim finally said, "You wearing me out. You ain't giving up. You gotta join us." That was how I ended up joining a black gang that had about thirty boys. Eventually, I rose to second in command. We were a rough bunch and did a fair amount of vandalism and got into street fights with other kids, but we never got involved in anything violent.

Years later, I was at Two Guys, the New Jersey discount store where I really learned to be a retailer. I heard a guy call out, "Bernie, that you?" It was Big Jim with some of his friends coming down the escalator as I was riding up with some colleagues. I got off and rode down to say hello. He was dressed in a heavy raincoat even though it was summer, gave me a big bear hug, and asked, "What are you doing here?"

I explained, "I'm an officer in this company."

Big Jim turned to his friends and said, "Guys, this is my friend Bernie. We've been robbing this place blind, but we can't steal from him." All of a sudden, they started pulling stolen merchandise out of their coats and pockets and put it on the floor. I heard rumors that he died years later in the electric chair in a prison in New Jersey.

In September 1939, the Nazis invaded Poland to start World War II. Those events would change the world forever—and the Marcus household as well. When the Japanese bombed Pearl Harbor in 1941, my two brothers left to serve. My sister worked for the government and married during the war. Her husband, Marty, served as a cook in the Army and came to live with us when he was on leave. Because she and I shared a room, my family set up a small army cot in the living room for me each night. I was twelve and already over six feet tall, which meant that my legs always hung off the end. But I didn't care because I loved my sister and was glad to have her close. Even as a child, I heard stories about how the Jews were persecuted. We heard terrible things on the radio, and I started reading stories in the *New York Times* and *Life* about Nazi terror, the creation of the ghettos, mass deportations, and the building of the killing centers. Everyone followed the news closely, and it became clear to me that had I lived where my parents had been born, I would likely not have survived. If they had not left Russia and the Ukraine, I probably would have been killed in a concentration camp. But I never understood why—my parents, our family, and our friends were all kind, hardworking people. Why would anybody want to kill us?

SON OF A BITCH

At age eleven, I started working regularly as a grocery store clerk and at a candy shop. I swept, stocked shelves, cleaned toilets, and did anything to make a couple of bucks. My father's shop was next to a dairy, and I got a job churning butter by hand. I also worked at a soda fountain. I was very popular among my friends because I would give them an ice cream sundae but only charge them for a soda. When the store closed, I walked over to the bowling alley and set up pins. On weekends, I worked at the Adams Theater as an usher. I took just about any job I could get. My parents were barely surviving, and they had no time to worry about me. I had to figure things out and solve my own problems and use my *sechel*—common sense—to make a way out of no way. I had to do it myself, and that included finding my own entertainment. I loved sports, so I would take the train, bus, or subway to Dodger Stadium, Giants Stadium, Ebbets Field, and Yankee Stadium alone. I never had enough money to buy a ticket, so I would walk in behind a man in a trench coat or slip under the fence. At a game at Yankee Stadium, I was sitting next to a priest. It was a no hitter, and Ted Williams hit a foul pop fly that was caught by the opposing team. The father screamed out, "Son of a bitch!" He turned to me red-faced and said, "Sorry, son." To this day, I don't know if he was happy or mad.

When I was still a teenager, we moved to a bigger apartment on Willoughby Street. It was in a nicer neighborhood, but what I remember most were the radiators. I had never lived in an apartment with heat before—they were noisy, but finally, we were warm. That year my parents became United States citizens, and I remember my mother coming home and crying like a baby. They had struggled so much to flee eastern Europe and were so proud to become Americans. My mother sat us all down in the living room after the ceremony and declared, "From now on we speak only English. No more Yiddish." My father was not convinced, but my mother put her foot down. "Joe, you are going to do it, or you don't eat." That day taught me the importance of embracing new opportunities without forgetting your past.

I had my bar mitzvah at the age of thirteen, but it was nothing like today. For the two years leading up to the event, I had to walk alone to synagogue to practice. In my second year, we moved out of the predominately black neighborhood where I had protection from my own gang to a new house, and I became the target of the Martini gang. This band of Italian boys, intent on abusing me, beat me up every Saturday. I never told my mother, sister, or rabbi what happened. Our local dentist would stitch me up if the cuts were deep. I jumped fences, hid in alleys, or tried to take alternative routes—and as a result often didn't make it to synagogue. On the day of my bar mitzvah our whole family walked together to the service. It was the only time I ever remember arriving without bruises or a bloody nose. I was wearing a used suit and my brother's old shoes. I never had a pair of properly fitting shoes as a kid, and to this day I still have trouble with my feet. There was no party afterward—just a few tuna fish sandwiches at the synagogue before we walked home.

I STARTED WORKING AS AN USHER AT THE MOSQUE Theater (now Newark Symphony Hall) at 1020 Broad Street when I was fourteen. It was built in 1925 by the Shriners as the Salaam Temple. But everybody called it the Mosque. I had never seen anything like it—the building had Greek and Egyptian motifs, marble columns, and a huge chandelier. It was a great job because I got to see all the performances for free. I worked with Seymour Levin, my buddy from Southside High School, and we saw the opera, ballet, and symphony. It gave me a real appreciation for classical music. We went backstage and met all the performers. Here we were, two poor kids who had never been anywhere, meeting famous people from around the world. After a performance we would sometimes head over to a local hotdog stand. The owner always let us go to the front of the line because we had on tuxedos. In a poor neighborhood, that really stood out. I think he thought we were important.

The Martini gang followed me to high school, and I remember one particularly brutal beating on the corner of Bergen Street and Clinton Avenue. I had finally had enough and went back to visit my old neighborhood to tell my black friends what was happening. We worked out a plan where I would challenge the leader of the Martini gang to a fight at the railroad yards. It was like something out of *West Side Story*. We both said we would come alone but knew that was a lie. He brought his whole gang, and my friends showed up with wrenches and baseball bats. We walked away from that fight with ten Italian guys on the ground, and the leader of my former gang told them, "You touch Bernie again, and I'll kill your whole family — your sisters, brothers, aunts, uncles, and cousins." That ended it. Years later, when I was visiting my old neighborhood in Newark, I found myself on that corner again and was telling the story to Jay Kaiman, president of the Marcus Foundation. I looked up and there was a Home Depot across the street. We could only shake our heads and smile at the irony. You never know what is literally just around the corner.

I attended Southside High School, which was founded in 1914, and loved it. Southside was integrated—fifty percent African American, thirty percent Jewish, and the rest mixed between Polish and Italian. I loved sports, and a small group of boys, including Artie Blidenberg and Ritchie Brinkman, created a ragtag football team. We just pulled together what we could and ended up with one helmet, a torn set of shoulder pads, a pair of cleats, and a ball for all of us. This was not an official team, but we somehow arranged a game against Irvington High School's junior varsity team. They were fully equipped—playbook and all—while we had nothing. At one point in the game, we managed to tie the score, but we were all bloody and eventually lost the game. I also joined the swim team; we did not have a swimming pool at the high school so we had to travel by bus to a local indoor facility to practice. Southside could not afford uniforms, so we swam at practice and in local meets naked, as did all the schools in Newark. It was not a coed team, so there were no girls. I did the backstroke in the medley with three other boys who did butterfly, breaststroke, and freestyle. We made it to an all-state meet one year, and that is when the school had to find us some swim trunks.

The teachers both loved and hated me. I could make anything into a joke, and I loved talent shows. The senior class at Southside gave two awards right before graduation—most likely to succeed and most popular. They asked me which one I wanted, and I chose most popular. The truth is, I had more fun in high school than should be allowed. At my graduation, in 1947, I cried.

IT WAS JUST BECOMING TOO DANGEROUS

I held multiple jobs and hustled my way through high school—never losing sight of the fact that if I was going to become somebody, I had to figure things out on my own. While working as a stock boy for Hahne's department store in Newark at the age of fifteen, I met a French girl whose boyfriend was the maître d'hotel at the Concord Hotel in upstate New York. I had terrible allergies, and she used to tell me that they would clear up in the Catskills. Those mountain summer resorts, in what was commonly called the "Borscht Belt" or the "Jewish Alps," were popular among affluent Jews throughout the Northeast from the 1920s through the 1960s. Think *Dirty Dancing* crossed with *The Marvelous Mrs. Maisel*. The two biggest and best-known resorts—the Concord and Grossinger's—offered Jews a place to socialize and escape antisemitism, if only for a brief time. My friend's boyfriend got me a job at Kutsher's Hotel and Country Club near Monticello. I said I was eighteen and had three years of experience (both lies) and was hired as a busboy and assigned to work with a waitress from Brooklyn College. I had never worked in a restaurant or even carried a tray—so I had a lot to learn. We started at seven a.m. and finished around midnight seven days a week. I was already a skinny kid, and after a month of running around that dining room, I lost fifteen pounds.

We had a tough station, especially a group of butchers who used to yank my chain. One would order something, and I would run back and get it. Then the next guy would order the same thing. Then a third guy would order it again. Instead of telling me all at once, they watched me run around like a rabbit. But I came to love the job and taking care of people. And I developed a pretty good comedy routine to boot. I eventually went to work at the Western View Hotel in Ellenville and became a waiter. A lot of entertainers worked the Catskills in the summer when theaters were closed, and I would write down their jokes and try to imitate them. I sometimes served as the master of ceremonies for the evening's acts, and so the singers and comedians would sit in my section. Sometimes they listened to my schtick and gave me a few pointers.

I loved being on stage, and I moved from being a master of ceremonies to a stand-up comedian, but what I really loved was hypnotism. I already mentioned that I wanted to be a doctor and loved reading about psychiatry, especially Sigmund Freud and Carl Jung. One summer, I met a man from Brooklyn named Elliott who was a professional hypnotist and had come to the Catskills to perform. Elliott took me under his wing. He taught me that it was all in the eyes—you had to have a pretty powerful stare to be successful. At night, when the dining room was closed, I would practice with other members of the staff until I got pretty good at reading and understanding people and their vulnerabilities. I was a shy kid with a stutter, and Elliott taught me how to use hypnotism to overcome it. I learned to slow down and think before I spoke, as well as use some of the calming techniques that I saw him use on stage. He showed me how to do individual hypnosis as well as mass hypnosis. It was a lot of fun, and my after-dinner show was very popular. I never tried to make a fool of anyone, and instead helped people find things they had lost or stop smoking. I once brought a couple on stage who had been married for sixty years. Under hypnosis, I took them back to when they met at the age of seven. They started speaking Russian, a language they had both long forgotten.

But then I had two serious incidents that scared me so much that I quit. One night, I put the band's saxophone player in a deep trance but could not bring him out of it. No matter what I did, he would not wake up. It eventually took me ten hours to get him back to normal. After that, I had to be careful not to make eye contact with him in the dining room. I also had a friend that was constantly tormenting me by saying that hypnotism was not real, that it was all a gag. He finally agreed to let me try to hypnotize him in the car by clasping his hands together. After a few minutes, he was in a trance and could not separate his fingers. When he realized that he was stuck, he started to panic and put his arm through the window and cut an artery. My other friends jumped out of the car and left us both while blood was spewing everywhere. I tore off my shirt, made a tourniquet, and raced him to the hospital. Right there in the waiting room, I decided that I had to stop—it was just becoming too dangerous. That incident taught me that when you have power, you have to use it responsibly.

I lived in the Catskills for two months each summer. Because we had no expenses—housing, meals, and uniforms were provided—I saved up nearly $2,000 each season, which would later help me pay for college. I learned a lot being on my own—I liked people, had a pretty good sense of humor, had enough chutzpah to take care of myself, and had a little talent. But mostly I learned that I was not afraid to try new things and take some big risks. Those skills were going to serve me well.

CHAPTER 2

HOW TO GET INTO BUSINESS

My failure as a hypnotist in the Catskills did not diminish my interest in medicine. I still wanted to be a psychiatrist. I figured I would attend Rutgers for my first few years then transfer to a university with a medical school. I had enough money saved up from working summers in the Catskills to pay my tuition and lived at home those first two years. I completed a lot of my pre-med courses, and in my second year applied for a medical school scholarship. I came to know the dean and was thrilled when he called to tell me that he had secured a scholarship for me to go to Harvard Medical School. I could not believe it. Then he said, "Here is the address where you send the $10,000 check."

What check? My stunned silence on the other end of the line betrayed that I had no idea what he was talking about. He finally explained that Harvard had a quota: only so many Jews could be admitted to the medical school each year. I later learned that this started in the 1920s, and by the time I was applying in 1949, the system was deeply entrenched and would stay that way until the 1970s. I would have had to bribe my way in.

This was old-fashioned antisemitism at play. I knew it all too well. Before the 1920s, there were few restrictions on medical school admissions, but as Jews entered the profession in larger numbers, non-Jewish doctors became concerned about the influx. In the early part of the century, applicants submitted their name, address, age, place of birth, name of college, and years in college. Starting in the 1920s, they were asked to list their religion and place of birth of their parents and submit a photograph. When criticism was raised about the new requirements, a new category—racial origin of the applicant—was added. That was eventually dropped and replaced with mother's maiden name. Each addition was designed to identify and root out Jewish applicants. Yale, Harvard, Cornell, and other elite medical schools all made similar attempts. These admission policies forced Jewish students to turn to other fields like dentistry, optometry, podiatry, or pharmacy, all of which had less stringent restrictions.

The backstory didn't matter much. There was no way I could come up with $10,000—not if I worked fifty jobs, started robbing banks, or turned every member of my family upside down to shake money out of their pockets. Even with what I had saved up working the summers in the Catskills, I was still poor. But it wasn't about the money—I was *not* going to pay a bribe to get into a school that I was qualified to attend. Devastated that my dream of becoming a doctor was over, I quit school the next day and hitchhiked to Florida.

WE'LL TAKE YOU THERE

I did not say a word to anyone. I went home, packed my suitcase, and walked out the door. I stood on U.S. Route 1 for about an hour until an older couple who spoke Yiddish stopped the car. They told me they were going to Miami; I said "Me, too!" and jumped in the car. This is a moment of *beshert*—the Yiddish word my mother taught me for destiny—in my life. The couple offered me a great deal: "If you will drive, we'll take you there." It took us three days, and I told them my whole life story. They were so happy to have a chauffeur that they paid for everything: all my meals, gas, and hotels. I think I reminded them of their grandson, and they were glad to have the company.

They had a condo on Miami Beach with an extra room that they gave to me. It seemed like I was having a run of luck, so I got a job working at a hotel on the beach that was owned by the entertainer Arthur Godfrey. It was a restricted hotel—no Jews allowed—but because I had red hair and blue eyes, they hired me. The only person who knew I was Jewish was the headwaiter, and he wasn't talking. By then, I had a lot of experience, so I did not cause him any trouble. He used to take me to the horseraces and taught me how to gamble—all I really remember to this day is that the first five races were always fixed. I made a lot of friends, and we would hang out on the beach after work.

I recall that Henry Ford II, who ran the Ford Motor Company from 1945 to 1979, came in one night with an entourage of twenty people and demanded that five waiters with white gloves serve him. They ordered all kinds of fancy food and wine, and when the bill came, they left a measly $10 tip. The next time he came in, the entire staff walked out, and management had to serve him and pay the staff what he owed them from the last time. I knew that my time in Florida would not last forever. After three months, I called my parents to tell them I was coming home. I returned to Newark because they insisted that I go back to school, claiming I would never be able to make a good living without a degree. That was not negotiable;

education mattered in our family—everyone graduated from college.

Not getting to go to medical school was not a personal failure as much as a failure of the system. Still, coming back from Florida, I was crushed. In retrospect, I guess I owe Harvard a big thank you for denying me entry. It changed the trajectory of my life and allowed me to help people in a very different way, and on a much bigger scale, than I ever could have imagined.

WHO ARE YOU?

When I got home, I realized that I could afford either pharmacy school or dental school. I was admitted to both, and because they were in Newark, I could live at home and save money. I chose pharmacy. It seemed closer to medicine, and I felt like it still gave me a chance to become a doctor. The school was founded as an independent college in 1892 and merged with Rutgers University in 1927 as the Rutgers College of Pharmacy. It started in a building on High Street in downtown Newark and then moved to Lincoln Avenue in the north ward. I hated it from the first day of classes, and I do not think they liked me much either. In my first year, I had a good friend that I played bridge with, and one day the dean caught us when we were supposed to be in class. He accused us of playing for money and was about to expel us, but my friend had political connections and got our senator and the governor of New Jersey involved. They pulled some strings, and we resumed classes.

I got married in pharmacy school, and we came up with a plan. My wife would continue to work as a teacher, and I would find some way to make a living, in addition to my studies. I already knew how to work hard, but I trace my do-it-yourself philosophy in business to this moment. Like my jobs in high school, this wasn't born out of a desire for independence, but out of desperation. I could not wait to graduate to feed my family. I needed a plan, and fast.

First, I was hired by a food freezer company and worked there for a while. Then two of my co-workers started their own company and invited me to become a partner. They worked during the day while I went to class. I came in at five o'clock, and on weekends, and drove to stores all over New Jersey. I did a lot of sales and marketing for the company. We partnered with some meat purveyors in the area and sold a package deal—if you bought the freezer, we would fill it with a hindquarter of beef, all butchered and ready to eat. We made money by selling the freezers wholesale; the meat was just a way to attract customers.

It was a great business, but exhausting. I got home around three a.m., and never made it to my nine a.m. math class. At the end of the year, the math professor held a study session for the upcoming exam and all the students were gathered in the auditorium. His name was Dr. Heimlich, and he kept looking at me. Finally, he stopped his lecture, and said, "Who are you?" I was trying to blend into the last row, hoping he would not notice. But I was tall, had blue eyes and red hair—and it was not so easy to hide.

So I said, "I'm Bernie Marcus."

"I know the name," he said, but still had a confused look on his face. "I don't think I've ever seen you before."

"Well, Professor Heimlich," I said, "I just have one of those faces. Everybody seems to forget me. It's been like this all my life. I show up, and nobody remembers me. It's like I'm invisible."

Feeling some sympathy, he said, "Oh, I'm sorry." And he continued with the study session. After I passed the exam, I went to see him in his office and confessed. He was really nice about it, and asked, "Why didn't you tell me? I could have helped you."

With school, work, and my growing family, I never had time to rest. I was a member of Rho Pi Phi, and members of the fraternity took notes in class. I would study them on the weekend for a few hours to keep up with the classes. It was hard, but I had a good memory and managed to survive.

While still in pharmacy school, I joined the New Jersey Air National Guard, and two weeks from finishing my junior year, my number came up. Not sure what to do, my friend Eddie Adams and I went to meet with the dean of the pharmacy school. We explained we had been called up and were scheduled to report for basic training in Mississippi to prepare to deploy to Korea. We asked if we could miss the last two weeks of class and still get credit for the whole year. He explained that this was not possible, so we went to talk to the commanding officer. Eddie and I were both good students who wanted to serve our country, but we also wanted to get credit for the hard work we had done in school. I could not afford to pay for an extra year. The commander was a great guy and was sympathetic to our plight. We offered to finish the two weeks of school and pay our way down to Mississippi to join our unit for basic training. He said if we could persuade the master sergeant of the plan, he would support it. The sergeant, however, was a really miserable guy. When we explained our situation he said, "You Jews are all alike. You don't want to serve your time like the rest of us and are trying to game the system. You are going into a MASH unit on the front lines, and I hope you both get killed." The commanding officer finally intervened, and we were able to finish the year and join a different unit.

Ironically, that sergeant's antisemitism probably saved our lives. Eddie and I were trained as medics, which had one of the highest casualty rates because they were unarmed and on the front lines. Two weeks after our transfer out of that unit, they were called up and suffered a terrible casualty rate.

We were never sent to Korea, but I served with the 108th Wing, a unit of the New Jersey Air National Guard stationed at that time in Newark, for four years. We were divided into three units: the air base group, the maintenance and supply group, and mine, the medical group. There, I met Pinkus Tabak, a farmer from Lakewood, New Jersey. He was a World War II veteran and the most decorated soldier I had ever seen. But he was also crazier than hell. We served every two weekends and did maneuvers once a year for two weeks. Eddie and I trained as medics, and Pinkus was a pilot. Once, while on assignment at Newark Metropolitan Airport, Pinkus was sitting in a fighter plane right next to our ambulance on the tarmac. The tail of his plane caught fire and flames were moving fast toward the cockpit. We were all screaming for him to eject, but he took his sweet time, waiting until the last minute. When he finally got out, we asked, "What took you so long?" With soot all over him, he just smiled. "How exciting was that!" I also remember once during a training exercise that he flew under the George Washington Bridge. But my main memory of Pinkus was that he was terrified of needles. We had to administer injections to our unit—everything from flu shots to vaccines—and every time Pinkus saw a needle, he passed out. So I did something that I was not supposed to do—I would give him a sedative to put him to sleep and then give him the shot.

I was almost expelled a second time from pharmacy school during my final year, and it involved a professor of a mandatory business class. He was a real schmuck, and everybody hated the course because he only talked about the theory of business. He was an academic, not a businessman. It was obvious that he had never worked outside of the university in his life. It was a complete waste of time. One day, I was so fed up that I finally said, "I'm running a business, and I can tell you that this course is worthless. Most of us are going to have our own pharmacy one day, and we need to know how to write a business plan, read a balance sheet, prepare a budget, hire people, and plan inventory. We're not learning any of that." As you might imagine, he was pissed. Even though this was a one-credit course, it was a graduation requirement. He gave a final exam one week before grades were due, and then quit—but not before he flunked three-quarters of the class out of revenge. That meant none of us could graduate, and it created quite a scandal. After dozens of parents complained to the dean, we were allowed to take another exam. We all passed and graduated.

KID, GET ME A CIGAR

I interned at several pharmacies after finishing my degree, became a registered pharmacist, and was hired by Dave Terry who owned Terry's Drugs in Verona, New Jersey, a wealthy neighborhood about twenty-five minutes north-west of Newark. Terry's was started in 1939 and was a specialized store, where doctors called the pharmacists to discuss a patient's symptoms, and the pharmacists wrote the prescriptions. It was a great place, with a lot of mer-chandise out front. It was interesting work because we had a direct line to the doctors, but I discovered that I really liked the retailing part. Dave was a wizard with vitamins—he had great displays and sold more than any-body around. But I wasn't at Terry's for long. Soon after I started there, my friend Larry Wortzel's father died, and Larry offered me a fifty percent stake in Central Discount Drug. His father's store was in Millburn, about ten miles west of Newark near the nature reserve South Mountain Reservation. This was not a good partnership, and I knew it from the beginning. You have to trust your instincts and partner with the right people, otherwise they can undermine any chance at success.

One day, I caught a kid who was stealing, and I grabbed his arm and said, "Don't ever come in here again. If I see you in this store, I will whoop your ass." The next day, he came in with a man I guessed was his father. He was as big as an NFL linebacker.

The guy said, "Where's Bernie Marcus?"

I answered, "That's me."

He continued, "This is my son, and you threatened him yesterday."

With gathering anxiety, I said, "Yes, I did. He was stealing from our store."

The guy went on, "Well, you have my permission to kick him in the ass if he ever does it again."

We both laughed and got to talking. It turned out he *was* a pro football player: Alex Webster of the New York Giants, who played in the NFL from 1955 to 1964 and later coached the team from 1969 to 1973.

Larry and I were not suited to be partners. That much was clear to us both. One day after we had a big fight, I was working late. A man, not much older than me, came in and said, "Kid, come here and get me a cigar." I was in my white pharmacist coat, was having a pretty bad day, and was no kid.

I turned to him with a scowl on my face and barked, "Pick a window!"

Baffled, he said, "What are you talking about?"

Angrier, I said, "Pick a window, because you are going through one of them."

He put his hands up in surrender and smiled, "I'm guessing you had an argument with your partner."

I was surprised because I had never seen this guy before, but he turned out to be Danny Kessler, one of our biggest customers. He owned United Shirt Shops and had been in the store before, but I had never met him. We sat down and talked for more than an hour, about my background, about the store, and about how much trouble I was having with Larry. He finally asked, "Bernie, what are you doing in this crummy store? You're smart. You love merchandising. You can do so much better. You should be working a concession in a discount store. I do men's clothing in a lot of different stores, and they are very profitable. You have to come see it."

I WAS EXCITED, AND DANNY AND I SCHEDULED A TIME to meet at the Great Eastern Mills store on Route 17 in Paramus the next day. Their first store opened in 1956, and eventually expanded to a chain of three stores in New York and New Jersey before the chain was bought by

Diana Stores Corporation in 1961. I had never seen a discount store or really understood what a concession was. I felt like a kid walking into his first candy store. Merchandise was everywhere—they sold home goods, clothing, cosmetics, luggage, furniture, and toys. I quickly learned that a concession was a store within a store, focused on a brand or a type of product, that was run by an entrepreneur. I saw some great merchandisers who really knew how to showcase their wares. Danny introduced me to Henry Flink, who ran the cosmetics department.

We talked for a while about his department, and I finally asked, "How can I get into this business?"

Henry smiled. "I can get you in."

Even though I had no money, Henry found me a place at Spears Fifth Avenue on 34th Street, right near the Empire State Building. Excited by the new opportunity, I went back to meet with Larry. He was not interested, so we finally agreed that he would run the drugstore, and I would take the concession at Spears. Henry helped me get started by selling me merchandise on credit, and I soon became his competitor. I knew that success was going to depend on how hard I worked. I had learned that lesson in the Catskills and in pharmacy school, and it was the same thing here. I had to find out what healthcare products and cosmetics the customers needed, then had to figure out how to buy them at a good price, and finally merchandise them back to customers in an appealing way. You had to be careful with manufacturers because they liked to fix prices, and if they thought you were undercutting them, they would refuse to sell to you. So I had to come up with some pretty creative deals. I was successful at first and even managed to expand to a second concession at Webster's. But Spears was not doing well, so when my friend Bob Silverman told me about Two Guys and how bad their cosmetic concessions were, I jumped at the chance.

I visited the Two Guys store in Totowa, New Jersey, about half a dozen times in a two-week period and found out that Bob was right. This is where I first learned how to walk a store and study your competition. Spears and Great Eastern Mills were good stores, but Two Guys was a great store. It was started by brothers Herbert and Sidney Hubschman in Harrison, New Jersey. They started by selling slightly damaged televisions before opening their first store in 1946 in an abandoned diner. They were so successful that other appliance dealers in the area began calling them "those two bastards from Harrison." Amused by the taunt, they changed the store name to Two Guys from Harrison. It was later shortened to Two Guys.

The Totowa store was nearly 160,000 square feet and was packed with customers. But the cosmetic department was terrible; it was disorganized, the products were out of date, and they had sloppy displays. I walked up to one of the employees, and said, "Who runs this place?" They pointed me to Herbie Hubschman—a man who would become one of my most important mentors. Not realizing he was the founder and CEO, I set out to introduce myself: "I'm Bernie Marcus. You have a great store. I'm in retail, and this place is terrific." Pleased by the flattery, he took me around the store for the next hour, walking in and out of each department and explaining where they got the merchandise, how much he sold, and how much profit they made. Two Guys had more than fifty percent of the appliance business in the region, a number that would grow to seventy percent by the late 1960s. I finally took him by the hand and said, "Herbie, you're a genius. This is a great store. Look how innovative you are and how many customers you have. But look at your cosmetics department. How could you operate a piece of shit like this?" I have to say my question surprised even me.

Embarrassed, he finally confessed, "Look, my brother runs it."

Seizing my chance, I replied, "That's the problem. If you let me take over and run this, I will pay you rent equal to the sales you are doing now." I had no clue how I would do it. Now this was not chutzpah, it was desperation. The pharmacy and Spears were doing well, but had a mountain of debt, and I knew I needed a new job fast. Dumbfounded, Herbie said, "Are you kidding me? You can't possibly make that deal." But I knew I could double or triple the sales, and I saw a chance to take a big risk. After negotiating some more, he and his brother, Sidney, finally agreed to come see my cosmetic department at Spears.

Revlon lipsticks were our big sellers. We bought them for seventy cents and sold them for a dollar and ten cents, undercutting our competition. I knew a guy in the beauty supply business and was able to purchase his inventory way under market. We made a killing, so much so that Revlon hired private investigators to follow me all over the place and tap my phone to find out how we were able to buy the lipsticks so cheap. Herbie was impressed, and after he and his brother got into a fight he said, "I can't give you the whole department, but I can hire you. I'll pay off your debt from Spears and Webster's and pay off the pharmacy debt to Larry, but you have to come work for me for three years."

It was—as Don Corleone might say—an offer I couldn't refuse. I had just learned that the man who ran the concessions at Spears stole all our money, so we were in even worse shape than I thought. Herbie offered me a good salary, and I brought my sales team from Spears and hired Herbie's nephew, Gary Hubschman, who was a crackerjack retailer. Pretty soon, I had taken over another department at Two Guys, then another.

This is where I cut my teeth—it was like taking a retailing and merchandising master class. No business school curriculum could have matched my time working in the store, talking to customers and buyers, training new employees, and trying new ways to sell more merchandise. My approach back then can be distilled down to one simple idea—don't sit back and wait for someone to tell you what to do. Pay attention to people who are successful, ask questions, make a plan, and do it yourself. I knew I had a lot to learn, so I had to find out how to get the skills and experience that would help me keep my promise to triple sales. I was passionate about understanding every aspect of the business, and I was not afraid to try new things. Some things worked, most didn't, but I knew I had to keep trying. Each mistake taught me something important, and within three years, I was running hard goods for the whole chain—everything but food, clothing, and toys. I was twenty-eight years old and was doing $1 billion in business.

I sometimes wondered how different my life would have been had I paid that $10,000 bribe to Harvard. There would be no Home Depot. There would be no Israel Democracy Institute. There would be no Georgia Aquarium. A lot of cutting-edge research on stem cells, autism, cancer, integrative medicine, and PTSD for veterans would remain unfunded. I am not one to look backward and become mired in regret, but I know one thing for sure: Do-it-yourself was my mantra.

WE ALL PANICKED

The biggest challenge I faced at Two Guys involved appliances, especially color televisions. We could never get enough inventory to satisfy customer demand. Two Guys was RCA's biggest customer, and we were lucky if we were able to get ten percent of what we needed. At the same time, we were buying more and more merchandise from Japan. I floated the idea that we should meet with the executives at Panasonic to see if we could persuade them to manufacture color televisions for us. I met with some of my people and the Panasonic sales representative and agreed that we should go to Japan to meet with the chairman of Panasonic. They started making black-and-white televisions in 1952, so surely they could do color. When we arrived, we made our pitch: "We really need color televisions and cannot get enough inventory. If you will consider manufacturing them, we can help you design it and commit to buy a certain amount, so you will not lose any money." We brought several RCA televisions with us to see if they could replicate the technology.

This was a yearlong negotiation, and we had to go

back and forth to Japan about five times. I traveled with Eddie Feldman, who oversaw purchasing, and Ed Fox, who managed the warehouses for Two Guys. Our Japanese counterparts were tough negotiators. They fought for every penny, but once you shook hands, they honored their word. Finally, we were close to finalizing the deal. Because we did not speak each other's language, we had to use interpreters, which made the whole process time consuming and cumbersome. But it also made it possible for us to talk confidentially without having to leave the room. Or so we thought. In the closing stretch of the negotiation, our progress had stalled; they seemed to be anticipating our every move.

Finally, I started to suspect that someone on their team spoke English. We were about to make an $8 million deal, and they had understood all our discussions that we thought had been private. We had to change tactics. We were three Jews from New Jersey—we started to speak in Yiddish! All of a sudden, there was a panic in the room. The entire Japanese team started talking at once and the negotiations were suspended. All we were told was that the chairman was ill.

For the next three days, we had to entertain ourselves— we went out to eat, toured the sights, and even went to the hot steam baths. I made quite a sensation because the Japanese had never seen a redhead naked. They had a hard time containing their amusement at my expense. On the fourth day, we were back at it, and I got right to the point. We were haggling over a dollar per unit—I suggested that we split the difference. If they did not agree, we were going to jump back on the train and leave Osaka. Within half an hour, we had a handshake.

The news traveled fast. On the train back to Tokyo, we were going to pass Mount Fuji and wanted to take a picture. Trains in Japan are famous for never getting off schedule, but the engineer was told who we were so he agreed to slow down so we could get a good photograph. The next day, we learned that every train in Japan had been disrupted. We screwed up the whole schedule, and it was all over the news. But Panasonic became the first Japanese manufacturer of color televisions for Two Guys.

About six months after we made the deal, I ran into the Panasonic salesman we had negotiated with in Japan in an elevator in New York. He had left the company and invited me for a drink. He had been part of the deal-making process and explained what had happened. He said, "When you all started speaking that new language, we all panicked. After we ended the negotiations, we held a big meeting to figure out what to do. We finally found a linguistics professor who determined what you were speaking, so they spent the next few days trying to locate a Japanese man who spoke Yiddish. You may not have noticed him when the negotiations resumed, but when you were discussing leaving amongst yourselves, he translated the threat, and the Panasonic team agreed to your terms."

TWO GUYS WAS A GREAT GIG, BUT IT WOULD NOT last. Herbie died in 1964. His brother Sidney had left the business the year before, and the three guys now running it were not qualified to be at the helm. The company was ultimately crushed by unprofitable acquisitions and over-expansion.

One miserable, snowy day in 1968, my windshield iced over while I was driving to work. I pulled onto the shoulder to clear it. While working on the side of the road, a car breezed by and splashed a puddle of freezing, slushy water over my head. Angry, dirty, and soaked, I decided I had had enough of this job. "That's it!" I shouted, to no one in particular. "I quit!" Not long after, Madison Avenue came calling.

CHAPTER 3

YOU CAN'T BUY PEOPLE

Toward the end of my time at Two Guys, I briefly considered going to work for the cosmetics company Fabergé. They had a pretty interesting story: The American oil billionaire Armand Hammer collected Fabergé pieces—ornate eggs, silver, and fine jewelry—in Russia in the 1920s, and encouraged his friend Samuel Rubin to start manufacturing perfumes and toiletries. Rubin's family emigrated from Russia in 1905, and he long dreamed of becoming a violinist, but after hearing Jascha Heifetz play, he knew he'd never be that good. So he quit and started an import business. By 1937, Rubin was selling under the Fabergé name. After World War II, he settled a lawsuit to use the Fabergé banner, and continued to sell luxury items to high-end department stores. He sold Fabergé for $25 million in 1963 to George Barrie who was a terrific entrepreneur and ran the business for the next twenty years. George launched dozens of new cosmetics lines and hired celebrities—like Cary Grant, Roger Moore, Margaux Hemingway, Joe Namath, and Farrah Fawcett—as "creative consultants."

In the late 1960s, while I was running the East Coast business at Two Guys, George started wooing me. He would pick me up with his private plane and fly me all over the place to meet celebrities. We met Ella Fitzgerald in London and Jerry Lewis in Las Vegas. One night, Cary Grant invited me to dinner at "21," the famous New York restaurant that had been founded as a speakeasy in 1922. Women stopped at our table all night to throw their panties at him—it was quite a scene. Grant got all the attention, and I got stuck with the bill. I think George was hoping that I might be dazzled enough to join the company as president. But I am a pretty basic guy and wanted to be involved in a business that I could believe in. When I looked at their books, I knew it was not for me. George had friends who had never worked for Fabergé and even his son's horses on the payroll. I could only see trouble, so I turned down the Fabergé offer and gave my notice at Two Guys.

YOU COULD NEVER MAKE THESE NUMBERS

In June of 1968, about a decade before we started Home Depot, I was hired to be the president and chief operating officer at Odell, a manufacturing company best known for their brands Ty-D-Bol toilet cleaner, Tintex fabric dye, and Esquire shoe polish. It was a very good company, but I was a fish out of water. I had an office on Madison Avenue in New York City, and I had to wear a suit and tie every day. I had always worked retail, so going into manufacturing was a big change. Two years after I started, the company faced a hostile takeover by Joe Katz at Papercraft.

Now, Joe was a bastard. He did not like me from day one because he wanted the people that worked for him to be subservient. By this time, I had a lot of experience and was not easily intimidated. I am also a terrible politician— I say what I think and do not do well with bullshit. I had a great board that was supportive of what we were doing, and I thought that would insulate me from Joe. Was I ever naive. On Thanksgiving morning, Joe called me to say that he had bought one of my board members. I didn't even know you could do that! It was becoming clear to me that my time at Odell was over. I stayed another eight months before moving to California to become vice president for Daylin Corporation.

Daylin was a retailing conglomerate that had more than a dozen brands—Elliott's Drug Stores (bought by Revco in 1975), Disco Department Stores, King Clothing, London Drugs, Miller's Discount Department Stores, Gulf Mart, Shoppers World, H.C. Enterprises, Diana, Great Eastern Mills Discount Stores, and Angels Home Improvement Centers. By 1969, Daylin had fifty corporate divisions and subsidiaries employing around 13,000 people. That same year, they acquired Handy Dan Home Improvement Centers, a small hardware store chain founded in 1955 and based in Los Angeles. Daylin was a good company but difficult to control because they had so many divisions. I was the executive vice president of merchandising and coordinated the merchandising of hard goods, drugs, and toiletries for Great Eastern Mills—a direct competitor to Two Guys.

About six months into my time at Daylin, I found myself at a meeting in Palm Springs. Each division was asked to make a sales and profit projection for the coming year, and none of the presentations seemed even close to being realistic. When it was finally my turn, I got up and made up a number that was easily ten times what we were currently making in profits. The chairman said, "What the hell, Bernie, you could never make those numbers." To which I replied, "I know, I just made them up. And so did everybody else. This is all bullshit. Nobody can make their numbers because they are not grounded in reality."

Everyone in that room knew I was telling the truth — and it didn't make me any friends. Not long after that day, I was moved out of my position. I think they gave me the job overseeing Handy Dan because they were trying to get rid of me. If it succeeded, good for the company. If it failed, I was toast. I had been running a $6 billion business, now I was being demoted to overseeing just six stores. They thought a demotion would make me leave. So, here it was 1972, I had a lofty title and not much else to show for it. I had an ex-wife and two children. My new wife, Billi, had a son, Michael, and we did not have any real money. I was pretty upset about it but said I would take the job on one condition: I had to be given autonomy to build my own team. I wanted an independent board and a chance to hire my own lawyers, bankers, and financial people — I had to prove that I had what it took to run a company my way. I could do it myself. They agreed because they wanted some stability and hopefully a chance to turn a profit, and that is exactly what I offered.

What happened next was simultaneously tragic and lucky. My chief financial officer was a nice older man. One day, he started slurring his speech. He seemed to be having a stroke right in front of us. I knew the symptoms and tried to get him on the couch while we all called for help. But he never recovered and died, and we lost a good colleague. That tragedy led me to Arthur Blank.

A graduate of Babson College, Arthur had returned to New York to work for the accounting firm Arthur Young & Co. In 1967, he joined his family business, Sherry Pharmaceutical, which shipped medications to hospitals, doctors, and drugstores. In 1970, Daylin bought the company, and Arthur became comptroller of Elliott's Drugs in Griffin and Savannah, Georgia. Within two years, he was president and chief operating officer. In 1974, someone in Daylin's main office suggested that I consider hiring him as Handy Dan's chief financial officer. He moved to Los Angeles and started on July 8, 1974. I was sure they were sending him to spy on me, but that's not what happened.

MR. CHAPTER 11

I have always known my limitations. I knew by then that I was a good retailer and merchandiser, but I hated balance sheets, budgets, and projections. That was where Arthur shined: the financials. One of the keys to success is to really know who you are and surround yourself with people that make up for your blind spots. I had lunch with my new CFO three times a week to talk about every aspect of the business. Even though I was twelve years older than Arthur, we became really close. We were the ultimate odd couple, I the merchant and promoter, Arthur the numbers guy. Our personalities could not have been more different, but we complemented each other. That is how we built Handy Dan into the most profitable part of Daylin. It wasn't long before our six stores turned into eighty, and we had expanded into Texas, Arizona, Oklahoma, New Mexico, and Colorado. Most of our competition sold about $3 million a year; we sold $5 million. Our team created a successful operation that had good cash flow and offered investors a solid return on their investment.

Handy Dan was doing great because we built a great team and stayed independent of Daylin, but the rest of the company was going down the tubes. In 1973, they were operating seven hundred drugstores, home improvement centers, and discount stores—it was just too much. Aggressive expansion, intense local competition, and mounting debt in a high-interest-rate economic environment resulted in significant financial problems. To survive, the company began selling off underperforming assets, and in January 1975, they hired Sanford C. "Sandy" Sigoloff to turn the company around. Daylin filed for Chapter 11 reorganization the next month and was delisted from the New York Stock Exchange.

Sigoloff was legendary, and for all the wrong reasons. He openly and proudly compared himself to "Ming the Merciless"—the ruthless tyrant from the old *Flash Gordon* comic strips—so that gives you an idea what we were up against. He became infamous for his "slash and burn" management style that would eventually become popular in the 1970s and 1980s. He had a reputation for making creditors happy and nobody else. He ruined businesses and tried to destroy workers' lives. He seemed to take special delight in acquiring troubled companies, pushing them into bankruptcy, laying off executives and much of the workforce almost overnight, and making millions when the company emerged from bankruptcy. He taught me more about leadership than anybody else in my career because he showed me what not to do.

Over coffee one day, Sandy told me that he was not satisfied just getting rid of people. He wanted to punish them. He wanted to make them suffer. I hated his tactics and told him, "When you treat people like that, it comes back to haunt you. People are scared of you." What I thought might offend him actually made him proud. I could see that he really reveled in being a son of a bitch. No wonder they called him Mr. Chapter 11. Sandy was no dummy—he had a background in physics, worked for the Atomic Energy Commission, and later took leadership positions at Xerox and a number of other companies.

He planned to reorganize Daylin using his "Infamous Black Book," which detailed how he was going to get rid of half the employees and either close or sell most of the business units. Handy Dan was the only profitable asset in the corporation, which I thought would protect me. It didn't.

I did my best to work with Sandy, but I was not naive. I knew that all he cared about was Handy Dan's cash flow. We were independent from Daylin—not a subsidiary, but our own public company. When they needed cash, we charged them five percent interest. About eighteen months after Sandy took over, I was asked to present about Handy Dan at a Daylin board meeting. I did not know that discussing a succession plan was on their agenda, so when my presentation was over, I got up to leave. Several of the board members asked me to stay, and I listened to the conversation about who would follow Sandy for about fifteen minutes. Finally, one of the board members said, "I don't know why we are carrying on with all this hypothetical talk. We have the successor right here in this room—Bernie Marcus." The look on Sandy's face told me clearly that he did not agree, and I knew then that my days were numbered.

During this time, I received a call from investment banker Ken Langone. He made a name for himself in 1968, when he took Ross Perot's Electronic Data Systems

(EDS) public. My friend Gary Erlbaum, who used to run a Philadelphia-based home improvement store, Panelrama, was working with Ken and introduced us. Now Ken was a piece of work—tough, aggressive—but also smart and honest. That first call felt a little like drinking from a fire hose. But we ended it with an appointment to meet for lunch the next day. Ken had two goals—to explain to me how undervalued Handy Dan was and to tell me that he was buying 400,000 shares. Concerned about who was buying up our stock, Sandy asked for a meeting with Ken. They hated each other from the start, and it became clear to Ken that Sandy had no respect for me. Eighty-one percent of Handy Dan's stock was held by Daylin, but Ken had managed to purchase the remaining nineteen percent. Much to Sandy's dismay, this gave Ken some power, and set the battle lines for a conflict that would play out over the next few months. Hoping to broker a resolution, I persuaded Ken to sell his stock to Sandy, believing that my job would be protected because of Handy Dan's profitability. I was a complete fool.

On January 9, 1978, Daylin announced that it had acquired all the publicly traded shares—by that they meant Ken's. For the next three months, I later learned, Sigoloff was plotting to get rid of me. On Friday, April 14, 1978, Arthur and I arrived for a corporate planning meeting at the West Los Angeles office. Things did not go as planned. I knew we were in trouble when Sandy called me Mr. Marcus. I was fired first, then Arthur and comptroller Ron Brill. We were unceremoniously thrown out of the building. Sandy not only fired us but accused us of National Labor Relations Board (NLRB) violations that resulted in a complicated series of investigations by the Justice Department and the Securities and Exchange Commission (SEC).

This was, hands down, the lowest point of my life. I had never been fired before, and my first thoughts were about revenge. When faced with a low like this you reach a point where you realize there is a fifty percent chance that you are not going to recover. If you are lucky to come out of it, you are stronger and wiser. If you don't, a sense of failure can really consume you. Those who survive these kinds of career-crushing events usually do so because somebody stepped up to help. I believe in "do it yourself," but that does not mean do it alone.

LET ME SHOW YOU SOMETHING

Sol Price became my savior. He was a successful businessman who owned Price Club (which ultimately merged into Costco), and we had been friends for years. He was thirteen years older than me, but we still developed a close relationship based on mutual respect. We used to visit each other's stores and talk about retailing trends. When he heard what happened, he invited me down to his home in San Diego for dinner. Born in the Bronx to immigrant parents, he was a pioneer in the warehouse store retail model. Sam Walton, who founded Walmart, used to say that he borrowed more ideas from Sol than from anybody else in the business. At dinner, our conversation soon turned to Sigoloff and the possibility of me fighting those false charges. I remember telling him, "My contract with Daylin was worth a million dollars. Sandy broke the contract. I want to get back at him, so I'm suing him for that million." Sol listened as I vented for a while. Then he stood up.

"Let me show you something."

He walked me to a back bedroom of the house and opened the door. Inside, there was no furniture, but the room was filled with boxes and stacks of papers almost to the ceiling. He explained that these were depositions and other documents related to a contract dispute that he was embroiled in against a German company.

"I have been dealing with this lawsuit for three years now," Sol told me. "This is all I do. My son runs Price Club, and the money we earn goes directly to our lawyers. This is how you will spend your next five years if you get tangled up in litigation with Handy Dan. Why would you spend your life suing somebody? Why don't you just forget about it? Otherwise, you're going to end up with a room like this. You and Arthur are great retailers so be smart and walk away."

I left San Diego with his advice ringing in my ears. Sol was right: Fighting Sigoloff would have been like battling flypaper—the more you fight, the stickier you get. Even if you win a case like that, you lose—your time, money, health, career, and sometimes even your family. I found myself at a crossroads—either to fight these false charges and spend a ton of time and money on attorneys or to walk away. I chose the latter, and it was the smartest thing I ever did. I got up the next morning, called my lawyers, and said, "End the litigation."

As terrible as the experience was—and it was pretty terrible—I learned something important about who I was. I would never treat my employees, investors, or customers like Sandy Sigoloff did. He was a reprehensible man who showered those loyal to him with money and sought to destroy anyone who crossed his path. He believed that you could buy people's loyalty and trust—and I believed you had to earn it. When we set out to build Home Depot, Arthur and I did everything we could to create a company culture based on respect and compassion. Sigoloff was important to us—not because we respected him, but because we never wanted to be like him.

So here we were, broke and without a clear path forward. Being fired from Handy Dan made me feel like a failure. I felt humiliated, and I know it really upset Arthur as well. But with time I came to see how these setbacks educated, pushed, and empowered us to take risks, to put our dream into action, something we never would have considered had we stayed. Walking away from Handy Dan and the lawsuit prevented us from compromising our values.

I think how you respond to failure comes down to whether your fear is stronger than your passion. People driven by passion see setbacks as unpleasant, but inevitable challenges. What they know that quitters do not is that failure can be eaten in small pieces. We were not quitters, and we would be damned if a few bastards were going to get in our way.

THAT IS GREAT NEWS!

Ken Langone would play an outsized role in what happened next. When I called to tell him about being fired by Sigoloff, he laughed and said, "Bernie, that is great news! You just got kicked in the ass with a golden horseshoe."

I couldn't believe my ears. "Why?" I asked.

"This is the opportunity you have been waiting for.

Now we can open the store you talked about back in Houston. Don't view this as a negative."

All I could think was: How did he remember our conversation from so long ago? I had only made a casual mention of my idea for Home Depot and did not go into any detail. But Ken was pumped. "Let's go out and get some investors. We can go to the people who invested in Handy Dan. You tripled their money, so now they can invest in your new concept."

As this was all unfolding, Fred Zissu tried to get me to return to Two Guys. Fred was a lawyer, and Two Guys was his client early in his career. In 1959, he helped arrange the merger of O.A. Sutton Corporation and Two Guys to form Vornado. He became chairman of Vornado in 1964 and chief executive in 1971. He knew I was in trouble with Sigoloff and offered to pay my legal fees. Enticed by the offer, I agreed to go spend a weekend with him. While there, Fred gave me his chauffeured car so I could visit nearby Two Guys locations. At the end of the day, I realized that there was no way to save the company—the culture had changed. The employees only seemed to care about themselves, and it looked like there was a lot of employee theft. It was sad to see. I came back and told Fred, "Look, if you want to make a lot of money, let's make this a real estate company. Get rid of the retail stores and rent the buildings." He declined, and we parted ways, but not long after our conversation Vornado, the parent company, did exactly what I proposed. In late 1980, Vornado was taken over by real estate investor Steven Roth, who owned Interstate Properties, Inc. Roth saw what I did— the land that the stores sat on was worth much more than the stores themselves. It cost about $2 a foot to build the stores, and they could charge $9 in rent. Soon, they began closing Two Guys stores and liquidating the merchandise. They took a $20 million loss in 1981 and started leasing the stores to other retailers (including, later, Home Depot). They made billions. But I did not!

I called Arthur, and we agreed to meet in a diner in Southern California so we could talk. I had been working on the Home Depot concept in secret for several years, and the idea came from listening to our customers. Every day, they complained that Handy Dan did not have a large enough assortment of products, regularly ran out of inventory, and was not a one-stop shop. I knew there was a better way, and Arthur agreed. We just had to try it. We filled several yellow pads with ideas about how we could build a new kind of home improvement store (though we didn't have a name for it yet). I lived north and he lived south, so we just picked a spot in the middle. He really liked the idea, but after a few hours finally said, "Your numbers don't work."

I was surprised. "What do you mean they don't work?"

He went on to explain his concern. "You lowered the gross margin, lowered expenses, and it just doesn't add up."

In response, I asked, "What would make it work?"

"Higher volume," he said.

"Well," I kept pushing, "then put in that we'll do higher volume. I know we're going to sell a ton of merchandise. I know it is going to work. So just put in higher volume."

He shook his head no.

I tried again to make my best case. Again, no. This went on for about four or five minutes. Me urging. Arthur refusing.

Now we were attracting some attention, because soon I was red-faced and screaming, "Put in the damn number!"

And he was shouting back, "I can't! They won't work!"

Ever the accountant, Arthur flat out refused. But we didn't have time to waste because Ken had arranged for us to go to New York to meet with potential investors the next day. You can't just start a business out of thin air—and we did not have the kind of money it would have taken to bring our vision to market. This was not a mom-and-pop enterprise. We planned to build stores that were 75,000 square feet, more than twice the size of our nearest competitor, filled with thousands of products. This would be big, maybe even transformative, and we needed money fast. Remember, this was the late 1970s. There were not a lot of venture capitalists or angel investors lining up to help two middle-aged guys who had just been fired.

So, imagine the scene. Arthur was angry because he thought I was being dishonest. He felt like his professional reputation was on the line. I was mad because he refused to take the risk to think big. And the next day, we were flying cross-country to pitch a business plan that didn't really exist yet.

WE ARRIVED IN NEW YORK AND CHECKED INTO A fleabag motel—if you could even call it that. We didn't have any money and had to share a room. It was so small that in order to get to the bathroom, we had to open the door. That night we decided to walk to dinner. We ate at an Italian place and walked home talking about our future. We stopped at the *New York Times* building to watch a protest of some kind before heading back to the hotel. The next morning, we walked into the investors' office, and I pitched the whole Home Depot concept. I talked about high volume, low expenses, great customer service, projected profits, and how we were going to completely change the home improvement business. Ken Langone was there on the sidelines like a Greek chorus, chiming in to bring home the message. The investors knew what we did with Handy Dan, so I think they were impressed, and I could even see Arthur starting to get excited. I guess the whole thing worked because they agreed to invest $2 million. We couldn't believe it—our dream was about to become reality.

THIS COULD GO ON FOR WEEKS

But this introduced a new problem—we had money and had to set up the company fast. We incorporated in Delaware on June 29, 1978, two months after we had been fired from Handy Dan. I knew that we needed some real talent—hiring can make or break a young company. I was good at marketing, advertising, training, and buying, but I hated budgets and finances. So we made a deal. I would become chairman and CEO, Arthur would be president and COO, and Ron Brill would be our chief financial officer (CFO). Ron, you'll recall, was fired by Sigoloff the same day we were. He had been Arthur's comptroller and was really talented. With that leadership team in place, we had to decide where to start the company. We both agreed that we needed to be close to a big airport—so we looked at Boston, Los Angeles, Chicago, and Dallas. We never even considered New York because it was just too expensive. Arthur loved the South, and he suggested Atlanta. We learned that JCPenney had four huge Treasure Island stores that were going out of business that might work. But before we could do anything, we had to find a bank.

We started with the banks in Atlanta, but they would not give us a line of credit. We were unknowns, had recently been fired, and they didn't understand our concept. Then we tried New York, Chicago, and Dallas, where the father of one of our investors owned a bank. Same story. No luck. We would be sunk if we could not get a line of credit. Finally, I called Rip Fleming at Security Pacific. Rip had been our banker while I was at Handy Dan, and he was the straightest shooter you ever saw. We set up a time to meet, and I launched into it.

"Rip, my life is on the line. If we don't get a line of credit from you, we can't get this business off the ground. Everybody has turned us down."

He was skeptical. "Well," he said, "we have never worked with companies outside of Arizona and California. This would be a big risk for us."

Without even thinking, I said, "Look, I'm not leaving this office until you do this. I will be here day and night. You will have to step over my body. I'll pee in a cup. And I'm going to stink up the place because I won't take a shower. This could go on for weeks, you have to help us."

He was finally starting to see the potential of our idea and pitched it to his loan committee. They turned him down three times, but he told us not to give up hope. On the fourth ask, he got the loan committee to agree to a $5.5 million line of credit. That was our lifeline.

THERE IS A CODA TO THIS STORY. WHEN HOME DEPOT stock was splitting and we were the darling of Wall Street, I found out a few things. First, Sandy Sigoloff had gone to the Security Pacific CEO and told them that he would give them all of Daylin's business if the CEO signed a statement that said I got kickbacks when I was leading Handy Dan. Rip and the CEO walked out of the office, talked for ten minutes, came back in, and Rip reported that he said, "Mr. Sigoloff, you have twenty-four hours to move your business out of this bank. This is not how we do business, and we don't ever want to see you in our offices again." Sigoloff did the same thing with our advertising agency, but luckily I was close friends with the owner, and they, too, ignored him.

Years later, when Rip retired, I was the master of ceremonies at his celebration dinner. That night, I was seated next to the CEO of Security Pacific, who told me a story. "You know, when Rip came to the loan committee to try to persuade us to give Home Depot a line of credit, we said no three times. The fourth time, he stormed into my office, threw an envelope on my desk, and said, 'Fuck this! You don't need me. You need a computer. I quit.' Rip never curses, so I knew he was really serious. If he quit, all of our retail business would have walked out the door with him. So we agreed to your line of credit. Rip was prepared to sacrifice everything for you. The day we gave you that loan, we wrote it off as bad debt. We gave you that deal to keep Rip at the bank."

Rip had never told me any of this. Suddenly, I started to cry. The next day, I called Arthur, Ron, and Ken and told them what happened. At our next board meeting, we voted to hire Rip as a special consultant to the board of directors and pay him a salary for the rest of his life because he deserved it. We would never have made it without him. He worked for us for years, visiting stores, writing reports, and never said a word about what had actually happened. Sometimes success depends on a quiet hero. We were lucky to have Rip in our corner. Who knows what would have happened if he hadn't risked everything?

But I digress. After Rip helped us get the line of credit, things moved really fast. We hired a marketing company to help us develop the brand, and I am here to tell you that we were *this* close to being named "Bad Bernie's Buildall." Our logo was to feature a man in a prison uniform. You have to remember that this was the 1970s and lots of companies—like Crazy Eddie's, the consumer electronic chain—used outrageous characters to build their brand.

Thank god for Marjorie Buckley, one of our early investors. She and her husband were driving around one day and passed a train depot that had been converted to a popular restaurant. She started playing around with the word "depot" and came up with the now iconic name. It had a no-frills quality about it. I loved it. Don Watt, a Canadian branding designer, designed the logo and chose orange. I'll admit, I hated that orange at first, but finally came to appreciate how distinctive and recognizable it was. Lots of companies have iconic colors—red for Target or brown for UPS. But none are so bright that you can see them from an airplane.

We opened our first two stores in 1979 on Memorial Drive and on Buford Highway in Atlanta. By the end of the year, we had three stores, two hundred associates, and average weekly sales of $81,700. We went public on September 22, 1981, after opening our fourth store because we needed more capital to keep expanding.

I don't think we could start Home Depot today. Public companies are now surrounded by lawyers and accountants—so many that you can hardly get into the room. It's hard to make a decision or take a big risk. It is just too complicated. The free enterprise system—when it works well—allows two unemployed, middle-aged guys to succeed and in the process create jobs. I'm concerned about the next generation of entrepreneurs whose creativity and innovation is stifled by the current legal and regulatory climate.

But back then, things were a little different. When people ask me about our beginnings, I tell them that we put our heart and soul into it, and we were not afraid to take big risks. We built a great team that shared our passion to build something from scratch. We dreamed big, and in the next chapters, I'll share my secrets.

CHAPTER 4

LOOK FOR THE GOLDEN HORSESHOE

All good companies, causes, and entrepreneurs have one thing in common: They find holes and fill them. Before Home Depot, if a contractor was building a house, they had to go to nearly a dozen stores—for paint, plumbing or electrical supplies, appliances, landscaping materials, or lumber. Imagine all the time and trouble that it would take to find, purchase, and coordinate delivery of those materials to a job site. Even if you had great salespeople at your local lumber yard or hardware store, it was still a pain in the ass, expensive, and really inefficient to drive all over town to buy what you needed.

What if you could put all the home improvement supplies under one roof, cut out the middleman, and pass big savings on to the customer? We thought we could operate on margins one-third less than our competitors and change the whole industry in the process. And that was only part of the formula.

We then hired skilled, friendly people to take care of you. In the 1970s, there was not the same do-it-yourself culture that we have today. The average customer lacked the technical expertise or confidence to put in a kitchen sink or do basic electrical work, so they hired a professional. It was often expensive and time consuming. Enter our initial Home Depot associates. We dressed them in bright orange aprons so they were easy to spot, trained them on our products, and encouraged them to share their knowledge with our customers. If you wanted to learn to use a drill, put down a hardwood floor, or install a toilet, our associates could show you how. The orange apron became synonymous with expertise, which in turn helped demystify home improvement.

The third piece of the formula was to offer classes and clinics to educate customers on how to do home renovations themselves. This encouraged them to return again and again to get more supplies, ask for further guidance, or take another class. That was our value proposition—give customers low prices and a big selection, helpful associates, a chance to learn a valuable new skill that would save them money and give them a sense of accomplishment. That is how we launched a movement.

The secret to our success was our core belief in caring for our associates just like we cared for our customers. Many of them left good-paying jobs to take a chance on us, and we promised that if we went public, they would share in the company's success. The more we could empower our employees to be self-reliant and entrepreneurial, to feel like they had skin in the game, the more loyal they would become. That was the culture we built at Home Depot, and it made us a nation of do-it-yourselfers. Along the way we learned some powerful lessons: You need passion, a willingness to take big risks to fill a need, partners that share your vision, a recognition that failure is not fatal, and the ability to tell a good story that inspires others to join you. Those four things helped us build one of the nation's most successful and respected companies that, in turn, gave us enough money to really solve big problems.

HIRE RIGHT

We could not have started Home Depot without the right people—Arthur Blank, Ken Langone, Ron Brill, Rip

Fleming, Pat Farrah, and dozens of others. Everyone had their strengths. Arthur was meticulous and ran things like a clock. Ron, Ken, and Rip brought additional expertise and energy. I'm an idea guy who loves to roam around and kick up dust. And I found a great merchandiser in Pat Farrah. Pat was flat out crazy and yet still the best retailer I've ever seen. He was terrible at operations, but he knew what customers wanted. Before we hired him, I heard a story that he once hung Christmas trees upside down, just to try something fresh. I knew him from my California days, and he was one of our earliest hires. He helped us build the brand as much as anybody else.

The heart and soul of Home Depot was, and still is, the associates. One of the most important parts of our do-it-yourself culture at Home Depot was finding the right people. We wanted people with experience in the building trades—so we hired carpenters to work in lumber and master gardeners in the garden department. We tried to make sure each store had at least one licensed electrician and plumber. They were often older and became mentors to the other associates. I started calling them "Bernie's Boys," and we actually began a hiring program for those over sixty who might be a good fit for our stores. Hell, we were nearing our sixties, and thought we were a pretty good fit! This was in an era when older workers struggled to get a job. Their experience allowed them to share what they knew with fellow associates as well as provide practical advice to customers. We also did not hire somebody into management just because they had an MBA and rarely brought in store managers from outside. We tried to keep to a seventy/thirty percent rule—where most of our managers were promoted from within because they knew the culture. But we also wanted some outside talent because we knew we didn't know everything.

Ron Brill used to say, "Payroll is not an expense, it's an investment." Our associates were compensated well for their expertise and were promoted from within. We offered salaried associates stock options and gave hourly associates a chance to participate in the stock purchase plan. Ron believed that we should always pay above minimum wage. He regularly checked payroll, and if a manager was trying to scrimp somewhere, they got a call from Ron. Payroll was controlled at the store level, so managers had a lot of flexibility. Arthur and I decided early on not to take stock options but instead give them to the associates, an unusual move for top leadership. We believed that this approach gave everyone the opportunity to have a vested interest in the business so they could focus on cultivating customers and building lifelong relationships.

If strategic hiring was the first step, our bread and butter was training. Most CEOs give up training employees once their company has become successful. Not us. We believed that if new hires learned from the founders, they would fully understand our values. Every new manager and assistant manager completed an eight-week training session, with at least one week in Atlanta. The sessions in Atlanta were taught by the company leadership—Dick Sullivan led the sessions on advertising; Ron Brill taught finance. On Friday, they did the morning with Arthur and closed out the week with me. New associates took classes on the company's history and the basics of good customer service and trained on the job. Then they shadowed a department manager, learning how to order, stock, and sell and did ongoing product training. The most important thing we taught was how to help the customer be successful on their do-it-yourself project. We taught the difference between asking: "What can I help you find?" versus "What project are you working on, and what tools do you need?" The first question might help them get a hacksaw. They'd buy it, go home, and quickly realize it was not the right tool for the job. Who would they blame? Home Depot.

As we continued to expand, training took a lot of time but was worth it. When we opened our first stores in New York, I got a handful of calls from other retailers who asked, "Where did you recruit your employees? New Yorkers are not this helpful. This must be a cult because most New Yorkers don't give a shit about anyone." I always felt like the people who came to work for us were unique—they were creative, entrepreneurial, and really believed in customer service. They made us great.

We believed that everyone at Home Depot should have experience working in the stores, including lawyers, accountants, marketing executives, and human resources people. They unloaded trucks, worked in the parking lots, helped with inventory, and worked as cashiers for between three to six weeks. I once had a lawyer complain, and I finally asked, "How can you handle our lawsuits if you don't know how our business operates?" We used to insist that buyers and suppliers conduct their business in the stores, so they could see what customers wanted. We even invited our vendors to come to the store, grab an orange apron, and work with customers in the department where we sold their product. We also required that board members visit twelve stores every quarter to stay in touch with what was happening.

Ken Langone loved that—and relished telling a story about finding rats in a store. After asking some questions, he found out that it had been a problem for a few months, but that's not what bothered him. The problem was that the bureaucracy kept the associates from fixing it. Ken made one call, while the manager had been trying to reach the district manager and headquarters to solve the problem for three months. So, at the board meeting, Ken told the story and reminded us, "Bureaucracy is like weeding a garden. Just when you're done, you better go back and start again." That is why I used to spend about forty percent of my time walking through our stores, so I could cut through any red tape. I learned more on these visits than I did in any boardroom.

I loved doing "Road Shows"—visiting various stores and leading impromptu on-site classes for associates. I'd spend a whole day at a store building the kind of bonds that you never could establish from behind a desk. Arthur and I also did quarterly Sunday telecasts called "Breakfast with Bernie and Arthur"—part comedy routine, part training session—that could be seen in the stores. "Issues and Answers" sessions were a place for employees to make suggestions on improving the company. We wanted the associates to know that we were part of the team and that they could pick up the phone and call us anytime. We were Bernie and Arthur, never Mr. Marcus and Mr. Blank. To this day, I think the time we spent training and traveling to stores was the key to our success. That gave us the opportunity to talk directly to our associates—from the newest to the most seasoned—and invest in them. The training was constant and those who embraced it were rewarded with good salaries and benefits and plenty of room to move up in the company. That might explain how, when we opened new stores, 7,000 people would apply for 150 jobs. If you were just looking for a job, we might not have been right for you. But if you were looking for a career, sign right here.

During one training session in those early days, I asked everyone to introduce themselves. Most of the people in the group had come from Sears, Walmart, or the construction trades. We finally got to this older guy with gray hair who was Navy. I made some stupid crack about him swabbing the deck, only to learn that he was a retired commander on the first nuclear submarine to go under the North Pole.

I could hardly contain my curiosity. "So what the hell are you doing here?"

He smiled and explained, "I love hardware and have always enjoyed helping people. This is my dream."

It sure was. He became wildly successful in his second career and could not have been happier.

Less than ten percent of our associates were part-time, and many invested in the company. If you had a thousand shares of Home Depot stock when we went public in 1981, it would have been worth about $12,000. By 1993, that stock was worth $2.5 million. No surprise that there are thousands of Home Depot millionaires, many of whom started working for us right out of high school. Tom Taylor started as a parking lot attendant in 1983 and worked his way up to executive vice president for merchandising and marketing. I learned from working at Two Guys, Odell, Daylin, and Handy Dan that if you treat people well, they feel their work matters. And if you make them feel like they own a piece of the company, even better. Respect breeds respect. If they hate you or the company, they work against you. Same thing with customers. Nobody has to shop at your stores. You have to wake up every morning and wonder, "Who will destroy me today if I don't keep my eyes open?" That's why I spent most of my time in the stores and not holed up in some executive office.

We also capped our compensation. Once the company became successful, we could have taken huge salaries like a lot of CEOs do today—$20, $30, or $50 million—but we told the board that we wanted to cap it at $2 million and not take stock options. People always tell me that we could have been the wealthiest men in America. But I argue that this decision helped shape the Home Depot culture; without sharing the company's success with our associates, it never would have become the same company. And don't worry about us, we did just fine. Our job was to make our associates' jobs easier and serve customers, and the optics of taking a huge salary worked against everything we believed in.

Another component of our culture was to create a company where people were not afraid to speak their minds. Arthur and I had come from Handy Dan, and we were determined not to reproduce the culture of fear that Sandy Sigoloff took so much pride in cultivating. Our best ideas came from our associates, and we had the good sense to listen. They did not hold back. Once, when visiting a store in the Denver suburbs on a Monday, I didn't see any of the managers on the floor. What was going on? I did not have any executives with me, and I told the associates that nobody was going to get fired, but I wanted them to tell me what was happening. When one of the managers finally appeared, he said, "We have so much paperwork on Monday that it takes me all day to fill it out, and we have to take it home at night to complete it. We do reports for district managers, buyers, and regional managers. I can't be on the floor and get it all done."

Sensing their frustration, I said, "Okay, tell me about these reports. Which ones are important, and which are bullshit?" Boy, I got an earful.

Smiling I said, "Here is what I'm going to do. I'll go back to Atlanta and send every one of you a stamp—a bullshit stamp. For every report you get that you think is bullshit, stamp it, and send it to me."

Then I met with the district and regional manager and buyer and asked them, "Do you know how long it's taking a manager to finish these reports? Sometimes two or three hours each. How many of you actually read them?

Or do they just end up in a file somewhere?" We talked through each one and whittled them down to the most important ones. Problem solved.

ABOUT TEN YEARS AFTER WE FOUNDED HOME DEPOT, I was on a bus in Israel on a trip trying to encourage business leaders to support Yemin Orde, an organization founded in 1953 to provide help to immigrant and at-risk children aged five to nineteen. We were on a long drive, and the trip organizer encouraged everybody to get up and tell their story. This guy got up and said, "I made the biggest mistake in my life when I did not invest $2 million in Home Depot for fifteen percent of the company when I had the chance. Today, that investment would be worth more than $50 million."

I didn't immediately remember him, but it turned out this guy was an investment banker from Boston. Years earlier, I had almost thrown him out of my car.

We had been in a panic. One day, Arthur came running into my office sweating and said, "We can't make payroll. We can't pay our bills. We've got to close this deal, or we're finished." We had been meeting with investors for weeks to raise more capital, and on that day, I had toured this banker around the stores hoping he would buy a stake in the company. I was driving him back to the airport. Not wanting to betray our desperation, I kept the conversation flowing, when he finally said, "I'm interested in this deal but have some questions: Do you have company cars?"

I explained, "Yes. We buy them for our district managers because they travel so much."

Then he asked, "Does Home Depot offer health benefits?"

Confused as to where this conversation was going, I said, "Yes."

He went on, "Well, when I invest in the company, the first thing I'm going to do is cut health benefits, take away all the cars, and have all the executives and managers take a pay cut."

We were on I-285, which is the busy connector around Atlanta, and I jerked the wheel to pull the car across three lanes of traffic to the shoulder.

Red-faced, I screamed at him, "Get out of the car!"

I leaned over and opened the door and was starting to push him out while still screaming, "That is not how we treat our associates, and there is no way we'll ever do business with you. I would rather go broke than to have you buy into our company."

It was rush hour, cars were whizzing past at eighty miles an hour, and he was half in the car and half on the side of the road. He kept begging me to let him stay in the car, and I finally, reluctantly, agreed, but said, "Do not open your mouth. I don't want to talk to you again." We drove the rest of the way in complete silence. When we got to the airport, he jumped out before I could even stop the car. I sped away, never to see him again. Until now.

After meeting on that bus in Israel, we actually ended up becoming friends. I once asked him what he had been thinking that day on I-285.

He smiled and said, "I thought I was driving a hard bargain. It was the dumbest thing I've ever done."

That incident taught me that if you settle for less than your values you are dead in the water. To think: Were we really going to take people's insurance away? What kind of company does that?

YOU CAN DO IT. WE CAN HELP.

To make sure that everyone understood our philosophy, Arthur and I created a customer "bill of rights," which stated that "customers should always expect the best assortment, quantity, and price, as well as the help of a trained sales associate, when they visit a Home Depot store." These commitments, still on the Home Depot website, reflect the company's "whatever it takes" philosophy.

Right after we started the company, I was walking

a store and noticed that we did not have some critical plumbing supplies in stock. I alerted Dave Austin, the store manager, and he ran down the street to buy what was needed from a competitor to avoid disappointing a potential customer. We had our own urban legend—that was actually true—about another manager who took back a set of tires. A customer, who shopped at the tire store that was formerly on the spot where the Home Depot now stood, came in to return old tires. Larry Mercer took them back and installed the tires by the cash register as a reminder to everyone that the customer was king. In Baton Rouge, several employees learned sign language to communicate with deaf shoppers from the Louisiana School for the Deaf. On Long Island, we ran out of Black & Decker snake lights, so an employee called a nearby Home Depot, drove over and bought some lights with his credit card, went back to his store, returned the lights at the return desk, and called the customer to tell him that he had what he needed.

One afternoon, I got a call from a store manager asking for help. He said, "There's an older woman standing here with five dollars in her hand, she's got a hole in her roof, and the rain is just pouring into her house. She keeps asking me, 'What can I buy for five dollars to fix it?' I don't know what to tell her."

This was not rocket science. The customer had a need,

and the store had the merchandise. All that was missing was a creative solution. One of the things that made Home Depot different from our competition was that we empowered our store managers and associates to solve problems every day on the floor. We did not have a huge bureaucracy that needed layers of approvals. We encouraged our associates to think like entrepreneurs. They did not need our permission for every single decision. He did not have to call me. He knew how to fix it because we had trained him to do this exact thing. I understood his desire for validation—it's a safe way to cover your ass. But here is my ten-second tip: Dig in so you fully understand the ask. Embrace your power to solve it. Brainstorm possible solutions, no matter how outlandish. Then get out there and do some good.

So what happened? The manager and I talked for a few minutes and agreed that he should use this woman's request as a training exercise, which helped associates learn about new products and build team spirit. He agreed to supply the merchandise free of charge and assembled a team of associates who wanted to volunteer their own time to repair her roof. They needed the practice using some of the products we sold, and this seemed like as good an opportunity as any. Then he took it one step further. Her ask was simple—help me fix this hole. But her problem was much more complicated. In the end, we replaced her whole roof, added a porch, and repaired her gutters and windows. The associates received valuable training and felt like their work mattered. The woman got a major renovation and became a customer for life. That's a win-win.

There are hundreds of stories like this—where Home Depot associates and customers came together to solve a problem and, in turn, devoted their time and energy to making their communities better. These good deeds became a major part of our culture—and part of the company folklore. That is the company we built.

STACK IT HIGH AND WATCH IT FLY

We've always felt as if we did more for average people than Uncle Sam, Congress, or any president has ever done. We started Home Depot when Jimmy Carter was in the White House, and interest rates to buy a home were pushing double digits. We were deep into a recession that started in the fall of 1973, and inflation and unemployment were through the roof. There were serious gas shortages throughout the 1970s, and people were struggling. They were looking for help, and Arthur and I thought we could fill the niche.

Armies of baby boomers were building or renovating houses—but money was tight. We made it possible to fix your toilet yourself for $3.50 instead of hiring a plumber for $50. We lowered prices and made it easier for people to build their dream house by cutting costs by ten to twenty percent.

Take ceiling fans. If you wanted to buy a ceiling fan for your house in the early 1980s, they cost about $200. We started selling them for $29.95. So do the math—you need four ceiling fans, and we just slashed the price from $800 to $120. And we taught you how to install them. No wonder they flew off the shelves. I think we put a ceiling fan in every home in America. Same thing with track lighting—it used to cost about $4,000—with us you could do it for about $400. Those were huge savings that really added up. Every big warehouse store today borrowed lessons from Home Depot. Selling directly to the consumer from the manufacturer, without a middleman, became a cornerstone of our economy.

When we started, most retail products went through four steps—from manufacturer to distributor to wholesaler to retailer. Now look around—you have Costco, Best Buy, and other warehouse stores that cut out the middle two steps and allow consumers to buy directly from the manufacturer.

We did not train the managers and associates to hawk products, but rather to develop customers' confidence in their own skills. Prove to a customer that they can do the job, and they will shop at your store. In the late 1970s, people were hesitant to do it themselves, so they hired professionals to do home improvement projects. I remember soon after we founded Home Depot, I was in the mountains having lunch. A dozen people came to my table to tell me about the kinds of projects they were doing around the house. My wife, Billi, and I could hardly eat! One guy, who was about sixty-five, was talking about how he was redoing the roof on his mountain cabin. I asked him, "When did you learn to do a roof?" He replied, "When you opened Home Depot!"

It wasn't enough for us to thrive; we wanted other companies to be successful as well. Pat Farrah knew the owners of Behr Paint, a small company in California. Not long after we opened, we went to meet with them. I brought pastrami sandwiches for lunch and talked with them about creating a national brand that would outperform Sears's paint. They had a great product, but we wanted it to be the best in the industry—second rate would not do. So, we did all kinds of analyses and refined the brand to create Behr Premium Plus. They became our in-house brand, and Behr was named the Home Depot Partner of the Year in 1984. In 1999, they were sold to Masco Corporation for over a billion dollars and are still our main paint supplier. The same thing happened with Emerson, which had an exclusive deal with Sears to manufacture Craftsman tools. For years, they refused to sell to us, but I wanted their product. Every year, I went to St. Louis to play golf with the CEO and make a pitch. Every year, he turned me down. One night at dinner, he told me that Sears was going to move their manufacturing operations to China and asked if Emerson could manufacture for us instead. It was a dream come true—they were so good and built additional factories. Emerson rebranded the tools as RIDGID for us, and it has been a terrific match. We helped these companies and so many more grow and thrive and saw that their successes helped our customers. That is how everybody wins.

THEY DIDN'T ASK PERMISSION

A central part of the Home Depot culture was the desire to help the communities we served, especially during natural disasters or national emergencies. Our proudest moments are when our people stepped up. When Hurricane Andrew hit South Florida on August 24, 1992, we lost a number of stores but still set up tents and temporary buildings to serve as command centers for first responders and relief agencies. I called the governor's office and told them that we would send supplies if they could provide state patrol escorts to keep our trucks from getting highjacked. I actually went on television to tell manufacturers not to raise their prices. If they did, I threatened, Home Depot would no longer sell their products. We were serious and stopped working with a handful of companies over this very issue. People were desperate, and the last thing they needed was price gouging.

On the morning of the Oklahoma City bombing on April 19, 1995, we saw the same thing everybody else did—the Alfred P. Murrah Federal Building in a pile of rubble. I called the manager of one of the stores close by to see if any of our employees were affected and to find out what we could do to help. He wasn't there. So I called the other store, same problem. Nobody was there. I was furious and told the operator to have them call me as soon as they got in. Not thirty minutes later, the first manager called to explain what was happening. The moment they heard about the blast, they loaded all their trucks with shovels, wheelbarrows, tarps, plywood—anything they thought would be helpful. They didn't call the corporate office. They didn't ask for permission. They just made sure that generators were available and that the first responders had axes and search lights. Nobody asked them to come. They just showed up. That is the heart of our do-it-yourself culture. We gave our managers that kind of autonomy—it was up to them to find out what their community needed and when.

After 9/11, the only trucks allowed into New York City and close to the Pentagon were from Home Depot, delivering supplies. They needed lumber, and we were in the best position to help. I also remember hearing a story from Virginia Beach after a hurricane. A customer called our store to say that they drove by Home Depot and the associates were giving out free water, while the competition was selling it for $5 a bottle. We didn't send a company-wide mandate to do that—the managers just decided on their own. Since then, we have offered our stores storm preparedness supply checklists and disaster preparedness workshops that include guides and videos. We don't wait for storms to hit. Days before, we set up an emergency management and distribution center with pre-loaded trucks and moved essential supplies to danger zones. After each disaster, we review our procedures to see what we can do better next time. It still makes me proud that you can engender that kind of culture in a company and have it endure years after you have gone.

We formalized our giving through the Home Depot Foundation and commit millions to hundreds of nonprofits. Today, associates regularly volunteer hundreds of thousands of hours each year. Nobody told them to do that. It is not required. It is just part of our culture. The foundation also supports job training, and gave $50 million in 2018 to train 20,000 veterans, high school students, and disadvantaged youths in the construction trades. We do much of this under the radar because we don't care who gets the credit, but we try to encourage our competitors to do the same. If we can leverage our support and encourage others to join, then we have doubled or tripled the impact. We know that shoppers care about how companies spend their money—and supporting good causes builds lifelong customers.

Arthur and I had a series of core values that were part of the company from the beginning. We believed in taking care of our people, empowering our customers to feel confident that they had the tools and skills to "do it yourself," and helping our community. These shared beliefs helped us to protect the environment, source responsibly, dedicate resources to emergency relief efforts around the country, honor veterans, promote training in the building trades, and serve the communities in which we operate. In 2001, the year before I retired, Home Depot was named the nation's most socially responsible company. What could be better than that?

MAKING DUST AND RUNNING SCARED

What really set Home Depot apart was that we had an ongoing commitment to running scared. We never wanted to get complacent. Arthur had a poster of a cowboy that said, "If You Don't Make Dust, You Eat Dust." We had a ton of entrepreneurial energy, hated bureaucracy, and were evangelists for customer service. It worked, and we grew fast.

In 1981, Home Depot went public. By 1984, we were operating nineteen stores, with a 117 percent increase in sales from the previous year. In 1989, we opened our hundredth store, then went global with stores in Canada (1994) and Mexico (2001). Our twenty-year growth outpaced Walmart. By 2005, revenue was $80 billion, and earnings per share doubled from 2000 to 2006. In 2000, we had eleven hundred stores. Within four years, that number had nearly doubled. The best part is that growth was because of, not in spite of, the culture we created.

After retiring as chairman of the board, I was determined to put the same energy into supporting things that mattered. I already knew that any successful enterprise, be it a business or a worthy cause, depends on the same winning formula that built Home Depot. You have to have passion for your cause, your people, and your customers. You have to take big risks. You can't be afraid of failure, and you have to tell a good story that inspires others to join you. That worked at Home Depot, and I knew it would work with my giving. Entrepreneurs make the best philanthropists—because they have built something and are not afraid to dream big and get their hands dirty. "Do it yourself" is their mantra. As long as they are running companies and worthy causes, we'll all do just fine. That is the joy of free enterprise. But the minute we get a bunch of bureaucrats or Harvard Business School graduates who have never created anything or taken any significant risks, things start to fall apart. So, when I retired, I focused on giving with the lessons I learned from Home Depot in my toolbox. I was about to kick up some dust.

CHAPTER 5

THERE IS NO NINE-TO-FIVE

Right before we got married, Billi and I were sitting in my car on Mulholland Drive overlooking Los Angeles talking about our future. I wanted her to know what she was getting into. I have never had a nine-to-five job in my life. I was not going to be home for dinner every night, so she had to cultivate her own interests if she was going to be happy. I didn't have a position—I had a passion, and I needed people around me who felt the same way. At Home Depot, I used to have lunch with the spouses of the executives and managers, and I was always blunt—your husband or wife was going to miss some soccer games and holidays. But if they were motivated and dedicated, they could make enough money to pay for college, a new house, or support a cause they cared deeply about. If not, they should quit and join the post office. I learned long ago that you cannot start a company or persuade people to support something you care deeply about if you do not have a clear sense of why you are doing it and why it matters. You also have to be prepared to live and breathe it for ten, twenty, and sometimes fifty years. It is not enough to dream. Passion takes a lot of sacrifice. I saw it in business, and I look for it in the causes I support.

Finding your true calling is not easy—I didn't truly find mine until I was kicked out on my ass at the age of forty-nine. Not everybody has such an abrupt awakening, so you need to consider three things to help sharpen your thinking: draw on your strengths and values, focus on your vision without practical constraints, and get an insider's perspective. Don't start a company that depends on customer service if you are an introvert. Don't go to work with or for somebody who doesn't share your philosophy about how to treat people. Don't let time and money keep you from going big. Don't go into an industry you know nothing about—get a job with a competitor and talk to insiders to prevent yourself from making a costly investment of time and money. Don't ever think you can't do it yourself.

GET NAKED

Arthur used to have a poster outside the conference room next to his office. It showed a picture of a lion and a gazelle. The caption read: "Every morning in Africa, a gazelle wakes up. It knows it must run faster than the fastest lion or it will be killed. Every morning, a lion wakes up. It knows it must outrun the slowest gazelle, or it will starve to death. It doesn't matter if you are a lion or a gazelle: When the sun comes up, you'd better be running." Despite our success at Home Depot, we were constantly running. Sometimes we were the lion. Sometimes the gazelle. Either way, we were always looking over our shoulder.

We didn't go into this business to open a few stores, punch a time clock, and go home to have a scotch and eat meat loaf. We were never satisfied with the status quo. Arthur used to say, "If you take your eye off the ball, somebody takes the ball away from you." We tried new products, offered new services, broke into new markets, and spent very little time talking about what was going well. If you found yourself a fly on the wall at one of our meetings, you would think the company was going down the tubes. Ninety percent of them were dedicated to failures, what our competition was doing, and which stores were having what kinds of problems. Products and services came and went as customers' needs changed—furniture and motor oil were dropped in the early years, rental tools and trucks were added. The stores changed from year to year, sometimes from season to season. We felt that if we weren't constantly trying new things then we were going backward. Ken Langone used to say, "The minute we allow anyone to compromise our values because of potential economic benefit, we haven't got any values." And our main value was to do right by the associates and the customers. That required constant change. We had to run faster than our competition—have better selection, deliver the best customer service, offer the lowest prices, and give customers confidence through classes, informal tutorials in the aisles, and even kids' workshops to make sure they could finish do-it-yourself projects with pride.

Change, for us, often came from within. As mentioned before, Arthur and I created a culture where anyone could make a suggestion—and we'd listen. Sometimes things got a little wild. Two stories about Mike Modansky, our lumber buyer, illustrate my point. Mike was a huge guy, six-foot-two and more than 250 pounds. Built like a linebacker. He was a Vietnam Navy veteran, and his family operated Ajayem Lumber in Walden, New York. He knew wood and often joked that he had sawdust in his blood. He was at a budget meeting with Arthur in our old headquarters that was a renovated A&P grocery store. Arthur would review the numbers for the coming year, and then each department head would come in to present their projections and request the funds they needed. Our budget meetings could get pretty heated, and this one was no exception. For an hour, Mike defended his strategy for the upcoming year, and Arthur pushed back. You could hear the screaming all the way down the hall. But that's not the story—that came later that night when Arthur called Mike at home to tell him that he respected how strongly he felt about his approach and didn't want him to worry about the fight.

Arthur and I expected our people to speak up because we valued their opinions, even when we disagreed. Lumber was one of our biggest sellers, and at each sales meeting, Arthur would tell Mike to "get naked" because lumber sales were driving the whole company. Arthur wanted him to cut prices, and "get naked" became a kind of internal joke. So, at the annual budget meeting in November, Mike walked in to find Arthur and some other executives at one end of the conference table. There were no women in the room, so Mike sat down and started taking off his clothes—first his shirt, then pants, socks, and even underwear. This was not a pretty sight as you can imagine—everyone was laughing, and Mike was just casually giving his budget presentation stark naked. At the end of his pitch, he turned to Arthur and said, "Well, you told me to get naked, so I got naked." Mike's stunt showed that he knew he could take strategic risks to make his point. He sure knew how to get our attention. That was passion.

WE WERE ZEALOTS

The work at Home Depot was demanding, and a lot of managers worked six days a week, twelve hours a day. In the early years, Arthur and I clocked fifteen-hour days because there was so much to do. We were zealots for our vision, but there were plenty of people who got burned out. I remember Jim Inglis, who must have put in a hundred hours a week. One day, Jim took a sabbatical and just never returned. He joked that like Pecos Bill, he had jumped onto a tornado and rode it west. Pat Farrah, our brilliant merchandiser, had the same problem. He used to say, "I wasn't good at moderation. I worked more than I should. I drank more than I should. I did everything to the extreme." Pat left us in 1985 to work for a sporting goods company and came back a decade later.

Burnout was real, and we were sympathetic, but we also knew that if everyone busted their butt for the customer, the whole company would be successful. If Home

Depot thrived, so did everyone else. Associates who worked hard made a good living and built a nest egg. But it took sacrifice and a lot of missed holidays and family vacations. From the day we opened our first stores in 1979 until the day I decided to retire, I never took a day off. I often use this analogy to explain my personality. Cars have different gears, and I am always in fifth. I wasn't born with a setting for park.

Being CEO was incredibly fast-paced and stressful, and there were plenty of legal and financial headaches. We had federal, state, and municipal regulations to contend with, constant issues with suppliers and manufacturers, and challenges with logistics, supply chain, and expansion that were coming at us at about 150 miles per hour. By the mid-1990s, I was feeling the toll that this constant barrage was taking on me. I talked to Billi about stepping back and then discussed it with Arthur and the board.

They tried to shut it down. "Just slow down," they said. "Trim back on your schedule. You can take some days off or work part-time."

But I knew that wouldn't work—I would have felt like I was stealing from the company. I knew that if I couldn't bring sustained passion, energy, and stamina to leading Home Depot, I needed to pass the baton. There are no part-time CEOs. If I continued, they were going to carry me out in a box—maybe one made with Home Depot lumber and nails—but a box all the same. On May 28, 1997, I stepped down as chief executive officer, but stayed chairman of the board until 2002. It was now time to take all the lessons I learned from my life and apply them to my philanthropy.

It was a hard decision because Home Depot was my life, but I knew I needed to make a change. We had started the Marcus Foundation back in 1989 and retiring gave me the time to focus on supporting things I was passionate about. For some time Billi and I had been talking about how we could thank the city of Atlanta and the state of Georgia. We had all the money we needed, and our children were doing well. We wanted to do something big to show how much we appreciated the associates and customers that stuck by us in the early years of Home Depot and helped build our business.

My friend Yoel Levi, then music director of the Atlanta Symphony Orchestra, really got my juices flowing. We talked about a museum, an opera house, and a hospital. Yoel almost had me convinced to do a new symphony hall, but then he abruptly left Atlanta and became principal conductor of the Brussels Philharmonic. I never signed on to his plan because I wanted to create something truly for everyone—children, teens, and adults of all income levels. Most of the associates that worked at Home Depot did not go to the symphony, and I owed everything to the people who wore the orange apron. We wanted to repay their sweat and their commitment to our values. It had to be something big. But what?

A FISH STORY

In June of 2000 I was attending meetings for the Israel Democracy Institute, the organization I helped found in 1991 with former secretary of state George Shultz, and ran into Georgia governor Roy Barnes in the lobby of the King David Hotel in Jerusalem. Quite a coincidence that two Georgians would meet halfway across the world, but we were good friends and started talking. I offered to give him a ride back to the U.S. on my plane, and he accepted. The flight took about fifteen hours, so we had a long time to talk. I told him about my conundrum: "I want to do something for the people of Atlanta and Georgia but don't know what." So we played the game "what if." What if I do this, what if I do that? Finally, Roy asked me, "What do you like to do when you are not working? What do you really enjoy?" I thought for a while, and then it hit me. Big fish. I loved going to aquariums. No matter where I traveled for Home Depot, I would often take a break for a couple of hours and go to an aquarium. I especially liked octopi. Watching fish gave me a sense of peace.

For my sixtieth birthday in 1989, Billi and I took a trip to California with friends to play golf at Pebble Beach. Billi set up an excursion to the Monterey Bay Aquarium, later made famous by the 2016 Pixar film *Finding Dory*. We had dinner in front of the big tank, watching the diver feed the animals. I loved it.

As I talked to Roy, a traumatic incident that I had long forgotten came to mind: a boating trip I took as a teenager. I caught the most beautiful, iridescent sailfish and pulled it onto the deck. I was so proud of the catch and was basking in my achievement. All of a sudden, the crew crowded around and hit it with a baseball bat. It was terrible, and I never went fishing again. I hadn't thought about that incident for years. But in that moment, the memory flooded over me, and I said:

"Roy, I think I've talked myself into something. I am going to build a big aquarium in Atlanta."

His first reply was "But we are landlocked."

I knew the beach was five hours east and that the Tennessee Aquarium was two hours north, but that was all the more reason to build it in Atlanta. A lot of people never get to see the ocean. I could bring it to their doorstep. The health of our state is based on creating jobs and attracting tourists, and this would be a stimulus for the convention business, hotels, and restaurants. I had found my passion. Now it was time to take my own advice and draw on my strengths—I knew how to build things. Focus on my vision without practical constraints—think big. And get an insider's perspective—this was going to require some research.

I was not the first person to float this idea. For over a decade, developers in Atlanta had been talking about building aquariums in tourist hot spots like Stone Mountain Park or near Turner Field where the Atlanta Braves played at the time, but they never materialized because funding was always an obstacle. When my plan was first announced, there were thirty-two aquariums in the United States and at least six in the planning stages, including ones in Portland, Maine, and Salt Lake City, Utah. Some, like Chattanooga and Baltimore, did well, but others, like Colorado's Ocean Journey in Denver, which faced a default on $57 million in bonds, had not.

I had something different in mind. This was not a public-private partnership. This was not a loan. I was going to donate $250 million and build the Georgia Aquarium debt free so that it wouldn't be in the red on opening day. We created a 501(c)3 and would not take any tax revenue from the city or state. This guaranteed that when we opened, we would have a positive cash flow.

Now, I could have written a big check and handed the whole thing off to a project manager. But I was determined to build the best damn aquarium in the world using the lessons I learned from Home Depot. When we got back to Atlanta, I pitched the whole idea to my board at the Marcus Foundation. They thought I was crazy because we usually focused our philanthropy on children, Jewish causes, medical research, the community, and entrepreneurship. Ken Langone said, "Bernie, this is your money, you can do what you want, but you're nuts!" Maybe I was. This whole fish tale is a book in and of itself—and you don't have time for that. But I want to tell you a few stories that illustrate how we merged passion and persistence with our belief in "do it yourself."

WHO'S GOING TO TELL BILLI?

We knew nothing about how to build and run an aquarium, and nothing about how to bring hundreds of thousands of fish to Atlanta. So we rolled up our sleeves. We set up a war room on the twenty-first floor of Home Depot headquarters and covered the walls in white boards and paper to workshop our ideas on everything from tank sizes to filtration systems to water quality. This was do-it-yourself on steroids. We brought in dozens of consultants and experts to help develop the initial plan. If the team had a problem, they called me. There was always a fight between the creative people and the fish people, but hashing out these issues behind closed doors helped us work out the kinks.

We had a vision, one not bound by tradition. I hated hearing "we can't do this" or "this has never been done"— that was a quick way to get thrown off the team. We were going to do something new, and we had to consider and test every idea, no matter how crazy. The trash cans overflowed in the war room. For every twenty bad ideas, a good one emerged. How things had always been done is not good enough. I wanted new ideas, not to recycle old ones. A lot of things that didn't pass muster ended up on the cutting room floor. We wanted visitors walking through the aquarium to never get tired of saying "Wow!" If it did not knock your socks off on opening day, we would have failed.

Rick Slagle, the Marcus Foundation's executive director at the time, became the project manager for the first year, and he helped assemble a team of consultants who had expertise in design, construction, and marine life to help guide the early conceptual phase. Our first official hire was Jeff Swanagan as executive director. And Rick wasted no time recruiting top-notch talent and an advisory dream team, some of whom had already been in the war room meetings. Once the skeleton crew was in place, we hit the road. I knew we couldn't build the best aquarium in the world without getting to know our competition. I used to do the same thing at Handy Dan and Home Depot—you always learned a lot from a good field trip.

Between the fall of 2001 and the spring of 2002, Billi, Jeff, Rick, and I visited fifty-five aquariums in thirteen countries, traveling a total of 109,000 miles. We visited the Florida Aquarium in Tampa, the Shedd Aquarium in Chicago, the National Aquarium in Baltimore, and dozens of others. We found the best sites in Asia, especially in Japan, Taiwan, Singapore, and China. They had amazing features: exotic fish, gigantic picture windows, and beautiful interiors that wowed visitors. No matter where we went, staff members opened their doors to us and talked honestly about their operations. We took notes, talked to staff and visitors, took photographs of everything. And we asked everyone the same big question: "If you had the resources, and could go back in time, what would you do differently?" The answers to that question would guide our work back in Atlanta.

But first, the logistics: The aquarium had to be debt free. We saw a lot of amazing institutions handicapped from the start because they were paying off construction costs. They rarely change their exhibits and programs because all the revenue was used to pay off debt. We were determined to use a business-based model to make sure the aquarium was cash-flow positive from the day we opened.

It was also very important to select a location that was connected to other tourist sites and part of the central city. We learned to design the aquarium from the inside out. Determine what animals and exhibits you want, then design around it. This project was about the fish, not the building, and operational efficiencies would be a core part of the design from the outset. That's why we decided to create an on-site animal health center that would include an operating room, laboratory, and pharmacy and staff it with top medical and veterinary experts. We heard about the importance of prioritizing conservation and education and decided to develop a robust education program for K-12 students that included a "learning loop" with a touch tank, science lessons, and a bird's-eye view of the biggest tanks and attractions. The final thing we learned is that aquariums are never finished. Plan for expansions, updates, and renovations from the moment you open your doors. This is the only way to attract repeat visitors.

The world tour had opened our eyes to what was possible, and Billi became determined to get beluga whales. Jeff kept saying that they were hard to import into the United States. Then we saw whale sharks in Okinawa, and we knew we needed them as well. These gentle giants are found in tropical waters and can grow as large as thirty-three feet. They are the biggest fish in the ocean and can live upward of a hundred years. Again, Jeff said, nobody has them in America. Only a few places in Asia have them. But we were persistent. "There is a way to do everything. Don't say no to me unless it is against the law. We have to make sure we can take care of them, but we are going to bring them to Georgia. And if we can't, 'Who's going to tell Billi?'"

At every stop, we came up with new ideas—dolphins, sea lions, stingrays, penguins, jellyfish—we had to find a way to make it work. I am sure Jeff was exhausted because he had to balance our requests with the complexities of bringing them to fruition. We wanted to build something that nobody had ever seen, but first we had to find some land.

LAND BEFORE WATER

A great facility needs a great location, and the hardest part about the whole project was finding the perfect spot in Atlanta. We had to have land before we could bring in water. We considered sites near Underground Atlanta, Six Flags Over Georgia, and Stone Mountain Park. We tried to keep the project secret, but as soon as people learned that I was in the market for real estate, the prices doubled and tripled. Now these were my friends, but they saw an opportunity and were prepared to take advantage of it. We had very specific requirements—we needed a large tract that was connected to other tourism sites and Atlanta's sports arenas. There had to be good parking and access to public transportation. Soon after we returned from Israel, on September 5, 2000, Governor Barnes and I met at the Governor's Mansion to continue our discussions about the project. Three months later, we met with Jim Jacoby who was developing Atlantic Station in midtown. By chance, Jim was also rehabilitating the country's oldest aquarium, Marineland, in Florida. The former Atlantic Steel site in midtown Atlanta was a brownfield redevelopment that was being reclaimed, and it was an exciting time. But in the end, it just didn't seem to be working. By late June, we were about to throw in the towel, when I got a call from Arthur Blank.

Arthur had some big news—Coca-Cola was planning to take a prime piece of real estate by Centennial Olympic Park and turn it into an amusement park with rollercoasters. I immediately picked up the phone to call Don Keough, president of Coca-Cola, who also happened to be on the Home Depot board. I thought this was a terrible plan that would cheapen everything around it, and I used the opportunity to extol the virtues of building an aquarium instead. During the call, he urged me to fly to New York to meet with Coke's chairman and CEO, Doug Daft.

On July 1, I jumped on a plane to make the biggest and best pitch I could—this aquarium would be great for the city. Coke could even build a new World of Coca-Cola on the property. It would stitch together the CNN Center, Philips Arena, the Tabernacle, and a proposed new children's museum. What an opportunity! I was there to really work him over with my great selling job, but after five minutes he confessed that he hated the amusement park idea, loved the possibility of having an aquarium, and even agreed to donate the land. I was shocked.

We announced the plan in August 2002, and Coca-Cola gave us 9.75 acres on the west side of the property that would eventually be renamed "Pemberton Place," after the inventor of Coca-Cola. We were elated; there was no better place in the city. This was, again, *beshert*— destiny. The site was a block from the fourth largest convention center in the United States and within walking distance of more than 40,000 hotel rooms. It abutted Centennial Olympic Park and was a stone's throw from the CNN world headquarters. The venues for the Hawks, Braves, and Falcons were close by, and there was easy access to rapid transit and to the interstates. The Georgia Aquarium had landed on the spot where it should have been all along.

THE BIG BANG

As we were finalizing the deal for the downtown site, we realized we had a big problem—we wanted to keep the details about the aquarium secret until opening day. I learned this lesson the hard way at Home Depot. If we were going to sell a hammer, we never advertised it until we had it in the store. It was like a Broadway play. Nobody sees the sets or costumes until the curtain goes up on opening night. We wanted a big bang—no previews, then suddenly *boom*! We would not reveal what fish we had until the time was right because we wanted to build the excitement and anticipation. Employees and construction workers had to sign agreements not to reveal what was coming. We also had lawyers blocking reporters from seeing the blueprints that were filed with the city's Bureau of Buildings, because they revealed trade secrets. Everyone knew we were building an aquarium, but the rest was a secret.

As you can imagine, this made the hiring process complicated. We could only talk in general terms about our specifications. We decided to work from the inside out, so our priority became finding the firm that would design the interiors. While we could not talk about the fish we planned to have on display, we felt we could share the basic parameters with the teams we interviewed. They were all confused by the secrecy, but we finally chose Jim Mookamp and Al Cross from the St. Louis–based firm Peckham Guyton Albers & Viets (PGAV). They had never worked in Georgia or on an aquarium, but had experience at Universal Studios, Busch Gardens, and Sea-World and understood how to use stage craft, theatrical lighting, and music to create unique, compelling spaces.

We all wanted a building that would enhance Atlanta's skyline, but not be the main attraction. I used to joke that I would fire any architect that won an award for their design. I wanted people to have to walk into the building to discover all the wonders and surprises. We explained to each firm we interviewed what we needed, but we could not tell them why. We said we need certain sized tanks, and they would argue with us. They kept saying, "You don't need it." The average tank size in an aquarium is ninety-five feet, and we wanted three hundred feet. Back and forth. So, we pivoted and started looking for firms who shared our passion for the project and were willing to take big risks. This was not so different from what we did at Home Depot. Buck convention. Try something unusual. Take a big chance. That is how we assembled an eclectic team—a designer, a Hollywood producer, an architect, engineers, and a contractor—who had no applicable experience and knew even less about the aquarium they were about to build. But full speed ahead. On

May 29, 2003, three years after that fateful trip to Israel, we unveiled the building's design and broke ground. Now for the hard part.

Getting construction permits in the City of Atlanta is like trying to build a pyramid on a tightrope. With one hand. Oh, and you're blindfolded. Our team repeatedly went back and forth to City Hall, but we could never get a straight answer as to when permits would or would not be issued. This is a pretty big deal when you have thousands of fish waiting for a new home. After a few months of this nonsense, I called Mayor Shirley Franklin and said, "I have to see you." I did not want to show our plans to anyone, but I needed Shirley's help. So I went downtown with the drawings tucked under my arm.

I said, "Mayor, I know that this aquarium is going to have a real impact on the city and state. It will create jobs. It will boost tourism. But we cannot get a shovel in the ground because of the city's bureaucracy. We are being held up by the permitting process." A light came on in her eyes, and she told me to wait and walked out of the room.

The next thing I knew, I was being summoned into a boardroom filled with her whole executive team. She said, "Ladies and gentleman, this is Bernie Marcus of Home Depot. We are building the largest aquarium in the world in record time with him. Nobody is going to stand in our way. I say this to every department—if you drag your feet on anything related to this project, you'd better look for another job." She put one of her managers in charge and instructed him, "You will carry the ball, and I will blame you if the permits are not issued in an efficient manner." Boy, that made a difference. The city hopped to it, and when we later had a problem getting a Certificate of Occupancy (CO) from the fire department before the whale sharks arrived, six months before the building was scheduled to open, she saved the day again. I called Shirley at City Hall, and she met me at nine the next morning at the construction site with the fire chief and told him, "I want somebody from your office on-site every day. If there is a problem, I want you to fix it immediately. I do not want to take any chances on safety, but I do not want to slow down for a minute."

Shirley changed everything, and we owe her a huge debt of gratitude.

FISH SHOPPING

How do you bring more than 100,000 fish, reptiles, corals, amphibians, and invertebrates from all over the world to Atlanta without anybody knowing about it? Very carefully. There is no aquatic equivalent to Home Depot, no single place we could grab an orange cart and go "shopping" for what we needed. Our goal was to acquire animals that needed rehabilitation or rescue or were bred in other aquariums or aquaculture farms. We worked with other aquariums, fisherman, and conservation groups all over the world to safely acquire what we needed. In some cases, we borrowed animals or received gifts, but more often than not we paid a steep price for the species we wanted to showcase.

Bruce Carlson, our vice president of education and an experienced diver, collected lagoon jellyfish in Palau in the western Pacific a year before we opened. We brought Asian small-clawed otters from a zoo in Paris. We rescued a hundred tarpon from a tidal pool along the Georgia coast. A school of cownose rays also came from Georgia, and six giant grouper arrived from a fish farm in Taiwan. We bought fish in February that were four inches long knowing they would grow to four feet by opening day. It was an expensive enterprise. The leafy sea dragon, a rare seahorse, cost hundreds of dollars a week to maintain. Multiply that by 100,000. You cannot believe how many state and federal permits we had to manage. We were awash in paperwork.

The most complex operation involved the whale sharks because they had never been transported by air. We literally constructed the whole aquarium around these beautiful animals. Late in 2002, we started design on the football field–sized exhibition—Ocean Voyager. Dr. Senzo Uchida coordinated meetings with the staff at the new Churaumi Aquarium in Okinawa to teach us how to best care for the animals. We now knew what to do, but we had no sharks. After thousands of emails and dozens of flights to Asia, we established contact with fishermen in Taiwan who located Ralph on February 2, 2005, and Norton on May 4. We sent a team to Asia to train them on how to live and thrive in their new habitat. Now how to get them to Atlanta?

It took dozens of people—speaking Mandarin, Taiwanese, Cantonese, Spanish, and English—to get the sharks into a net, lift them onto a moving boat, and deposit them in a fiberglass tank. The tank was designed for a long-haul journey, with a special life support system and window so the three biologists and the veterinarian could monitor their condition during the flight. We had code names, secret agreements, and cloak-and-dagger logistics that helped us get them from eastern Taiwan to Atlanta.

They arrived in Atlanta on June 3 in secret on a 747 cargo plane that was donated by UPS, for which we are forever thankful. The pilots had to do special flight training to keep the tanks stable and minimize the water sloshing around. They flew at 37,000 feet to avoid rough weather that might stress our precious cargo. When they landed at 6:03 a.m. at Hartsfield-Jackson International

Airport, their tanks were carefully loaded onto trucks and taken to the aquarium with police escorts. The whole operation was thrilling.

As the sharks were hoisted from the tanks thirty feet into the air and placed in their new habitat, we all held our breath. A whole team of on-site divers and specialists had been waiting for hours to assist with this single moment. Once Ralph and Norton touched the water and their massive, shimmering tails propelled them forward we all felt an intense sense of exhilaration and relief. These were rescue animals that were part of the annual catch allowed by Taiwan. If we hadn't purchased them and brought them to Atlanta, they would have ended up on somebody's dinner plate.

A few weeks later, we had a population explosion—giant grouper, batfish, sea goblins, and bowmouth guitarfish arrived on a MD-11 widebody airplane. The 8,000-mile trip left from Kaohsiung International Airport in Taiwan, stopped in Alaska to refuel, and sixteen hours later arrived in Atlanta. The whole operation cost more than $200,000, and UPS once again donated their services. The fish, water, tanks, and pallets weighed 147,000 pounds. In October, two beluga whales named Nico and Gasper, who had been rescued from a tank under an amusement park in Mexico City, arrived. Three females (Natasha, Marina, and Maris) from the New York Aquarium for Wildlife Conservation would join them right before we opened.

The most exciting part about bringing the fish was finding a way to showcase them—and the centerpiece was a huge acrylic window. Billi and I had seen one at the aquarium in Okinawa that made you feel like you could slip right into the deep blue sea. We negotiated with Nippura Corporation, and they designed the window in six separate segments, packed it, and shipped it to the Port of Savannah. Each piece weighed eighteen metric tons, was twenty-four inches thick, and had to be manufactured to exact specifications. We created a huge opening in the building with a perfect two-inch gap to allow for the installation. All of this had to happen before we put on the roof. We arranged a police escort from Savannah, knowing that if we chipped or broke any of the pieces of the window, we would be dead in the water. It would take months to remake and would delay the entire project. We watched a terrifying scene as the cranes lifted each piece and slipped it into the frame. It took hours to install a single piece. I still cannot believe it, but the damn thing was a perfect fit.

Installing the six pieces was only the first step. The seams were still visible, so now the real work began. They had to bond it together and seal it into the concrete frame. We built a plywood waterproof enclosure over the whole thing, and highly skilled Japanese engineers worked under it for three months to finish the window. Then the window had to cure at 179 degrees Fahrenheit so it could dry completely. There were no walls or roof, so we had round-the-clock security to safeguard the workers and our investment. Like us, Nippura wanted to protect their trade secrets, so nobody saw what they did. The final window weighted 119 tons and is one of the largest windows of its kind in the world. It is 74 feet long, 3 stories tall, and withstands 1.9 million pounds of pressure. The window helped showcase our Ocean Voyager exhibit that housed more than fifty aquatic species and is still one of the largest single aquatic exhibits in the world. I still have no idea how they pulled it off, but it is magical. I love watching visitors stand in front of it, especially children, who are simply mesmerized by the ocean life in front of them.

WEAR OUT

On November 19, 2005, at 2:07 p.m. we cut the ribbon to officially open the Georgia Aquarium. We projected that we would attract about 1.5 million visitors in the first year—that number topped out at 3.6 million. This was big. After the first year, I realized that it was time to step aside. My passion had become a reality, and our dictatorship was about to become a democracy. I was not jumping ship entirely; I would stay chairman of the board. Gratitude started this project. Passion fueled it, hard work made it possible, and good business sense ensured that it was sustainable.

Whether you are constructing a giant fish tank or helping build a house for Habitat for Humanity, you have to discover what you care about and find a way to do more of it. I don't think I have ever worked a forty-hour week in my life. When Arthur and I started Home Depot, we put our whole lives into it. So leaving it and deciding to retire was a big decision. I knew that I was getting older, but I wasn't done yet. I had worked since I was eleven, and I wasn't going to stop now. I loved retail because I got to work with people who thought on their feet, were sharp, and solved problems. But some of the best retailers and entrepreneurs I knew who made it big retired and never did anything else. I appreciate that you get tired—and some people find themselves forced to retire because of an illness or other family responsibilities. But those that still have energy, stamina, and wisdom should get involved with something else. I worked hard in my life—probably too hard. I had a heart attack, five bypasses, and my aortic valve replaced, but I decided long ago that I would rather wear out than rust out.

The world moves so fast. A hundred years ago, we

measured things in months and weeks. Today, it's hours and seconds. I have seen a lot in my life, but some things never seem to change. Hard work and free enterprise are the hallmarks of success in this country, and nobody knows that more than the child of an immigrant. When I look back, I am overwhelmed by a sense of gratitude. I loved building Home Depot, and I never imagined I could do anything more important than that. I'll bleed orange forever. Then I retired and jumped headfirst into philanthropy. I know I am lucky to have found so many other things to be passionate about—serving veterans, curing diseases, and giving families hope.

There are people out there every day doing similar things with the same kind of commitment—running a food bank, giving supplies to community schools, and inventing something that solves a real problem. They don't have millions of dollars. They are not CEOs. But they have the same thing I have: passion and a willingness to kick up some dust to make something happen.

CHAPTER 6

PROBLEM. SOLVED.

All good companies, causes, and entrepreneurs have this in common: They find problems and solve them. At Home Depot, we identified a need and met it and became more successful than we could have ever imagined. Customers loved it because they saw the immediate value—they found what they needed, got great service, learned a new skill, and saved money. That's how we invented "do it yourself." So what if you take that approach and apply it to your personal life, your business, or your giving? To do it right, you must answer two simple questions: What is the need, and how can we meet it? Identify the problem, and don't wait for your parents, your co-workers, your spouse, or the government to come up with the solution. You have to believe in your power to "do it yourself." Let me tell you how I did it in business and in giving. Maybe that will inspire you to do the same.

A VICTIM OF YOUR OWN SUCCESS

"Do it yourself" was a totally new concept in the retail hardware business in the late 1970s. We trained our associates to help, but there were only so many at each store, so we also added instructions to products on the shelves. If you went to buy laminate flooring, you found a sheet of step-by-step instructions right next to the product. But we soon realized we needed a more formal approach—so we started offering classes on wallpapering, installing a fence, painting, laying tile, building a storage shed. I had tried offering classes at Handy Dan, but it didn't work because they were taught by the manufacturers' representatives and felt like informercials.

We didn't just educate our customers, we changed the way people thought about their homes. Instead of hiring a professional for each repair, people came to us for help. In the 1970s, most people wouldn't have dreamed of buying a fixer-upper. By the 1990s, our customers did it all the time. We had given them the power and confidence to do it themselves. To build on this concept, in 1995, we published a book, *Home Improvement 1–2–3*, in partnership with *Better Homes and Gardens*, and it was an instant bestseller. That led to another book, *Outdoor Projects 1–2–3*, and a magazine called *Weekend*. Pretty soon we had a TV show called *HouseSmart* on the Discovery Channel. Our Kids' Workshops became really popular, and we have given away 85 million kits since 1997.

One big difference between our philosophy and that of our competitors was that we did not upsell. We were not McDonald's—we didn't ask you if you wanted to supersize your order. Our goal was to find out what problem customers were trying to solve—a leaky faucet? a broken window?—and then identify exactly what tools and skills they needed to complete the job. If we could help them solve the issue for $5 instead of $500, then we felt like we had succeeded. We didn't get that $500 that day, but we hoped to have gained a customer's trust, and they might go on to spend $50,000 in their lifetime. We treated our customers fairly, gave them the tools to be successful, and built long-term relationships. But we also empowered our associates to think like entrepreneurs. We encouraged them to take ownership of their part of the store. When walking through the aisles that sold ceiling fans, hardware, or electrical supplies, you might see signs that indicated that this area was proudly maintained by a specific employee. They decided how to merchandise it. They kept track of inventory. They took responsibility when something went wrong. They were empowered as well, and there is nothing more satisfying than knowing that your work matters.

Our success, though, brought new problems. One big issue started to undermine our ability to deliver great customer service—overcrowding. People could not find a parking space. They couldn't find a cart. They walked in and saw huge lines at the checkout, and they couldn't locate an orange apron to help them get what they needed. All of this threatened our commitment to customer service. We tried a variety of strategies to fix it. Some stores opened early for contractors, to help them get what they needed before the workday started. Some stores even stayed open for twenty-four hours. We also started opening stores near existing stores. Now this might seem like a counterintuitive solution—why cannibalize your own customers? But what we found is that as the sales growth for individual stores went down, the company's overall sales increased. The new stores kept the old stores from getting choked with customers. And if we put a new store on the periphery of the area served by an older store, we not only relieved its traffic, but courted new customers who would come to a more convenient location.

We needed to reorganize the stores, too, for a better shopping experience. We moved lumber from the back of the stores to the side and created registers close by to prevent other shoppers from having to stand behind huge carts loaded with wood. We widened the aisles to allow multiple carts to pass more easily and installed more vertical shelving to allow us to put more products on display. This kept customers from having to wait for an associate to go into the back to find the toilet they needed. We moved the kitchen, wallpaper, and bathroom departments to the back of the store, which gave shoppers a quieter space to plan major renovation projects. We added overnight shifts so associates could stock shelves at night, freeing them up to help customers while the store was open. When a single store is doing $60 million in sales, it is a major task to get inventory from the back door onto the shelves. We didn't want our associates to be so busy restocking that they ignored the customers. We also added new services like a wedding registry. We thought newlyweds might need a new lawnmower more than a set of silver candlesticks, and we were right. People loved it and filled their registries with hoses, paint, shovels—all the things to outfit a new home.

We also found that even though people loved shopping at our stores and doing projects themselves, they sometimes wanted professional help. In the early years, we installed garage door openers and not much else. But we noticed that some of our competition had created successful installation departments. If we were going to remain competitive, we had to fix this issue. We selected one store in Chula Vista, California, to do a beta test. We started offering to install windows, doors, water heaters, and other big-ticket items—and the impact was immediate.

But as we expanded, our legendary service started to suffer. The installers were not Home Depot employees—rather, they were outside contractors who were not trained in all things orange. They were late. They didn't clean up after themselves. They forgot to connect the wiring for a ceiling fan, and on and on. We had rolled out the service too fast. So we decided to cut back our installations to a few things—kitchen cabinets, heaters, carpeting, and garage door openers, and each store selected a list of preferred contractors that we helped train. We realized that if we focused on a narrower range of services that we did well, we would be better off than doing a lot of things half-assed.

Some people like to read reports. Others meet with their managers to get the pulse of a company. Arthur loved to study spreadsheets. I walked stores—going department to department, talking to associates, looking at merchandise, asking customers questions. I quickly learned that the best way to evaluate the quality of a store was to start in the garden department. It was the most difficult part of the store to keep clean and organized. You had a ton of merchandise that you had to keep from dying and all kinds of supporting products—from pesticides to mulch that had to be stocked and maintained. A hard freeze, an infestation, or a heatwave could wipe you out. A good garden department meant a good store. If it was a mess, so was the store. It was harder to hide problems in the garden department, so my research paid off. You can use the garden department in your own life. Research and study your own business or the cause you are considering supporting. It doesn't matter what it is—a local coffee shop, a $250 million aquarium, or cancer research. Dig in. Figure out what the problem is, and brainstorm creative solutions. Along the way, try to do some good.

BEN HILL

We really cared about our customers at Home Depot, but that doesn't mean we never had complaints. We just handled them differently than other companies. We learned early on that company executives who get too far removed from their core business lose sight of what is important, and that's when you start to get in trouble. I was inspired, of all things, by the Israeli army. In Israel, their generals, colonels, and majors lead their forces. They are on the front lines, not back in a command center. Their official motto is "Follow me." Leadership means sacrifice, and that's how we handled complaints at Home Depot. If someone called the corporate office with a complaint, it was patched through as a "Ben Hill" call—named by our merchandising guru Pat Farrah. Pat saw the name on an exit on the west side of I-285, the perimeter around Atlanta, between the Home Depot support center and Hartsfield-Jackson Airport, and thought it sounded friendly and would be a good nickname for complaint calls.

If a Ben Hill came in, that meant the highest-ranking executive got the call. It started with me, then Arthur, then Pat, and on down the line. We would actually answer the phone by saying, "This is Ben Hill. How can I help you?" We never told the customer who we were because we wanted them to tell us the truth and not be intimated by talking to an executive. Customers complained about long lines, that it took too much time to get what you needed and get checked out, that they couldn't find the item that was advertised, and that there was not enough help on the weekends. Instead of dreading Ben Hill calls, we welcomed them, because it told us that our customers had confidence we could fix problems. The calls were like informal focus groups—we didn't have to pay anyone to tell us what was wrong. Customers called us directly. We got and still get thousands of letters and phone calls—and each one told us what we could do better.

It can be hard to listen to criticism, but it's essential to improvement. I remember one customer who called about delays in a delivery that was holding up an entire construction site. I listened to the whole story, and said, "This is terrible. I have to fix it."

The man on the phone said, "Okay, who are you going to hand me off to?"

I said, "Nobody. This is my company, and I'm going to fix it."

Confused, he asked, "Who is this?"

I replied, "Bernie Marcus. I founded Home Depot."

He gasped and said, "Oh, Mr. Marcus. I'm so sorry to bother you."

I replied, "It's Bernie, no bother, and I am going to fix this." And I did.

We didn't farm out complaints—no third-party group handled it for us. We did it ourselves. As we grew, it became necessary to hire "Ben Hill" associates. The first one—Bill Sanders—was a manager from our Marietta, Georgia, store. He was "Mr. Customer Service." He helped assemble a great team, and even as the department grew, we never lost our interest in having direct contact with our customers. That was our philosophy—listen to the customer's complaints, try to understand the issue, brainstorm ideas, and fix it efficiently. Our job was to make every single customer happy, and we would not rest until the problem was solved.

The concept of Ben Hill is just another way to

encourage our associates to embrace the do-it-yourself mentality. We had Ben Hill posters with a man who looked like Pat Farrah dressed in an orange apron in each of the stores that advertised the number. We felt that putting a name and face on the complaint line would help customers feel comfortable reaching out.

Our "Ben Hill" associates had one job: focus on customer satisfaction. I remember one Ben Hill associate telling a story that reflects what I mean: "This woman called me one day and said her dad visited a store and had a bad experience. He was sick at the time, and I called to see how I could fix it. I learned that her dad's name was Homer (like our mascot), and he loved Home Depot. So I fixed the problem and then found a Homer doll and took a picture of the mascot when he was in the store and mailed them both to her father. She was really touched and called to thank me." That's a Ben Hill. You have to be all in—our Ben Hill associates used to say "Bennin' It to Win It." You can't quit until the customer is satisfied. Our approach was easy to replicate, and plenty of other companies have done so. Chick-fil-A always gets top rating in the American Customer Satisfaction Index (ACSI), and their employees are rated the most polite in the industry. Trader Joe's, Publix, and Apple are not far behind. It doesn't cost much to do the right thing, and I can assure you that you will pay plenty for getting it wrong.

All these stories are variations on a theme. We founded Home Depot to solve a problem: How can we create a store that puts everything under one roof so customers don't have to visit five or six stores when doing a home improvement project? While we were building it, we solved problems every day. Each one required that we admit what was wrong, brainstorm creative fixes, and pivot when necessary. When I retired, there was still a lot left in me. Our giving had been growing since we founded Home Depot, and I now wanted to give it my full attention. I strongly believed that the lessons we learned at Home Depot about solving problems could help. In my early years, we were reactive—if somebody approached the Marcus Foundation, we reacted and either gave a grant or not. Once we narrowed down to a handful of causes, we were determined to be proactive and try to solve big problems. But we weren't going to just donate money blindly and move on to the next project. We had time, talent, and treasure and were ready to get our hands dirty.

AN ABSOLUTE DISGRACE

Public and community health is a major concern for me, and that issue hits close to home. Dr. Jeffrey Koplan, then director of the Centers for Disease Control and

Prevention (CDC), came to my office to explain that the CDC was woefully unprepared for any kind of disaster and was struggling to attract top talent. He was making the rounds to major foundations in Atlanta, and so I was not surprised to see him at our door. He explained that the facilities were inadequate, and, in a crisis, the staff had to pull TVs into an auditorium and get their information from the networks. Can you believe that? Every television station in America had secure satellite phone technology, but the nation's top public health agency did not. This seemed crazy and revealed that we really had two major problems—we needed an emergency response center, and the three CDC campuses were desperate for some serious renovation. The September 11 attacks in 2001 and the anthrax scare of 2002 made the work even more urgent.

One issue at a time. In 2002, the Marcus Foundation donated $3.9 million for a new emergency response center and helped encourage more than a dozen companies to make in-kind donations or provide deeply discounted equipment. Along with Jeff's help, we did the whole project for about $7.1 million and completed it in less than a year. The state-of-the-art facility, near Emory University's campus, now enables the CDC to employ an integrated response to any health emergency. This helped create a secure communications hub that linked the CDC with the Department of Health and Human Services (DHHS), the

Department of Homeland Security (DHS), the federal intelligence agencies, emergency response officials, and local and state public health officials. The facility, named the Marcus Emergency Operations Center (EOC), opened in 2003, with eighty-five workstations, nine team rooms, a central command station, high-frequency radio support, and geographic information system (GIS) disease mapping capabilities. Finally, the CDC was well equipped to handle bioterrorism attacks or disease outbreaks.

It would have taken years to procure this equipment from the federal government, which is why I hate partnering with them. We had to act quickly, and the best way to get moving was to make a big gift and then call on America's corporate leaders to join forces to help bridge funding gaps. It worked, and the Marcus EOC was activated during the Space Shuttle *Columbia* explosion and the SARS outbreak in 2003, as well as every disaster since. We saw a problem, recruited great partners, and didn't wait for somebody else to do the work. The CDC would not have been anywhere near prepared to help with the COVID pandemic that began in 2020 had private companies and entrepreneurs not taken the initiative decades before.

Our 2002 gift set in motion a much larger renovation of the CDC. Jeff invited me, Oz Nelson of UPS, and Phil Jacobs of BellSouth to tour the facilities. We were stunned to see that the world's leading scientists were working in outdated and unsafe conditions that included termite-infested barracks from World War II. Some of the buildings on the Buford Highway campus in Atlanta were actually collapsing. There were tarps on roofs holding water off millions of dollars' worth of equipment. There were labs housing biological agents in rooms with walls that were close to the outside of the building, making them vulnerable to car bombs and other attacks. Wires were frayed, air handling systems were inadequate, and freezers and lab equipment were stored haphazardly in the hallways. We saw a refrigerator that employees used to store their lunches next to an unsecured refrigerator that held dangerous mycotoxins. If this had not been a government facility, it would have been shut down by the Occupational Safety and Health Administration (OSHA). One employee went to the ladies' room and fell through the floor because of the rotted wood. It was an absolute disgrace. We had to do something.

Oz, Phil, and I went to Washington, D.C., to lobby Congress to help complete the desperately needed upgrades. At first, we could hardly get a meeting with anyone. Every year, we made at least two trips. As the emergency center took shape, we started to get more attention, especially from Tom Harkin (a Democratic senator from Iowa) and Arlen Specter (a Republican senator from Pennsylvania). We were persistent and didn't want to waste any time or put up with any political bullshit. Our approach eventually paid off, and Congress increased the budgetary appropriations so that over an eight-year period the CDC received nearly $2 billion to renovate the main facility near Emory University, rebuild the entire Buford Highway campus, and help make repairs at Fort Collins. I would hesitate to get involved with a project like this again because the government lacks the kind of urgency that we feel is so important, except that it had such an impact on the welfare of the whole nation. The entire CDC project brought with it a powerful lesson: An early gift intended to fix one problem can be leveraged into additional corporate and federal support to solve an even bigger problem. We had no idea when we made our first gift and started working with the CDC that it would become such a major project. But we did know that we could not do it alone. It worked, and that's what I call success.

EMPOWER, DON'T PATRONIZE

The CDC posed one challenge, helping veterans was another. Our nation has been in a constant state of war since 2001, leaving more than a million soldiers suffering from invisible wounds, including PTSD, TBI, depression, and addiction. Nearly thirty American veterans commit suicide every day. This is more than a problem. It is a national shame. Veterans are underpaid, struggle to reintegrate into society after being discharged, and when wounded are treated as second-class citizens when seeking medical treatment. They are treated as if they are disposable.

My brother, uncles, and cousins all served in World War II, and some of them came home broken men. There was no treatment for what was then called "shell shock." Soldiers just tried to piece their lives back together and cope the best they could. I saw family members, and some of the men I served with in the New Jersey National Guard, struggle for the rest of their lives, so this was personal for me.

I am a very patriotic person. My parents were Russian and Ukrainian immigrants, and the happiest day of my mother's life was when she became a U.S. citizen. I take service to my country very seriously, and every time I see the flag or hear "The Star-Spangled Banner," I get a flutter in my heart. I am so thankful to be an American, so when I read another story in the newspaper about a veteran suicide or see a segment on television about how we are failing veterans it makes my blood boil. Those who need help often wait months to see a doctor, are told that the specialist they need is not available or covered by insurance, and then get trapped in the sea of red tape that has become the Veterans Affairs (VA). Their service and their time battling bureaucracy leave both visible and invisible scars. If you spend any time with service men and women affected by invisible wounds, you find out that every single one of them—from generals to enlisted personnel—has contemplated suicide. This is how desperate the situation is.

Like with the CDC, we saw the problem but had no idea how to fix it—so we did what I always did: took a field trip. This time I went abroad. Unlike here, in Israel, veterans are given a lifetime of support and honor. The U.S. and Israel talk about service and war wounds in completely different ways, which helps explain why the two countries have such dramatically different approaches and outcomes. When a soldier in the Israel Defense Forces (IDF) is wounded, an officer is attached to their family. The IDF sends them to the best medical facility anywhere in the world. They fly the family to join the soldier and cover all the expenses related to the treatment. When a soldier is killed, the IDF assigns an officer to the family who stays with them for the rest of their lives. On the anniversary of the soldier's death, the IDF comes to support the family.

Part of the reason this system works is because nearly everyone in Israel serves in the military—it is mandatory with few exceptions. The result of universal service is that everybody understands the rigors and risks and supports one another. Additionally, service and remembrance are built into the very fabric of Israeli life. The day before Independence Day (Yom Ha'atzmaut) is the Day of Remembrance (Yom HaZikaron), when fallen soldiers are honored. When discharged from the military, many disabled veterans in Israel join Bet Halochem ("The House of the Fighter"), which has rehabilitation and recreational facilities around the country. They serve with a community and are discharged into one. That is not how it works in the United States, where so many veterans talk about being isolated and abandoned.

This trip to Israel just confirmed what we already knew—our nation was not doing enough to help those who protect us. While running Home Depot, Arthur and I made sure that the company was friendly to veterans. During the wars in Afghanistan and Iraq, I regularly did "Breakfast with Bernie" broadcasts and remotely spoke with our employees who were serving overseas. In the corporate office, we had a wall that showcased our associates who were deployed. If their families needed help around the house—with a roof or plumbing—we sent a Home Depot team out to handle it free of charge. We offered military discounts to active duty, retired military, and reservists. We partnered with the Departments of Defense, Labor, and Veterans Affairs to create job opportunities for current and former members of the military. Home Depot and the Home Depot Foundation also committed funds to providing training in skilled trades and helping them find jobs in the home improvement industry. A number of veterans participated in the program in partnership with the Home Builders Institute (HBI), Construction Education Foundation of Georgia (CEFGA), and Atlanta Technical College (ATC). This might explain why, today, there are more than 35,000 Home Depot associates that are veterans, military reservists, or spouses. When they were called to serve, the company paid the difference in their salary while they were on duty. Since I retired, Home Depot has kept their promise to veterans, and my own commitment has only deepened.

I saw the challenges veterans faced in recovery while on a visit to the Shepherd Center in Atlanta. I tell the story of how that visit inspired my interest in helping start the SHARE program for veterans in the prologue, but *how* we did it is as important as *why*. Veterans come to Shepherd for a two-week evaluation—everything from their physical capabilities to their psychological state. Neurologists, psychiatrists, psychologists, speech pathologists, occupational therapists, and physical therapists treat them for eight to twelve weeks. This is intensive; they live in apartments close by and work eight hours a day, five days a week, and sometimes on evenings and weekends. The veterans also work with social workers, recreational therapists, and vocational rehabilitation specialists to help them strengthen and maintain their independence. When they finally return home, SHARE funds a case worker for them for the next two years.

Those who participate in the program have been amazed by the thorough and coordinated care; they had not seen anything like it at the VA. We know it has an impact, both from our detailed follow-up and from the letters we receive. Melissa Roberts wrote about her husband Dustin: "SHARE accepted my unraveling family. SHARE was there for my husband when I didn't know how to be. SHARE became a crutch to lean on, a whisper of hope that told us it was okay to not be okay. SHARE taught my husband the tools he needed to pick himself up again. This program helped my family find joy again." These kinds of testimonials explain why the SHARE program and its alumni have not reported a single suicide.

GO BIG

We loved SHARE, but it only served veterans who could come to Atlanta—that was not a success in my mind. We had to find a way to replicate it around the country. As a man on a mission, I went to Washington. I was determined to shame the Pentagon, the VA, and Congress into covering all the medical costs for veterans. I met with generals, members of Congress, and senators. At one meeting with the ranking officers for the Marines, Navy, Air Force, and Army, and staff from the VA, the Department of Defense, and the Surgeon General's office, I was told, "This is a great program. It's terrific. We'll pay for it." Famous last words—before I could even get out of the building, it was tangled in red tape, and I never got spit out of them. I always felt that if the VA were a private company, it would be out of business in a month. Our wounded warriors deserve much more than this, and I was not going to give up.

In 2013, the Marcus Foundation hired Marcus Ruzek and gave him a single mandate: "We want you to make SHARE a national network and really extend it. Don't be afraid to go big." We had interviewed a number of candidates for the position to manage our veterans' affairs portfolio, including some high-ranking generals. During the interviews, they kept referencing how "their staff" was going to take care of everything. Well, we knew right away that this was not going to work. We needed somebody who was not afraid to get their hands dirty. We found that person in Marcus, who had been recommended by our friend Army general Matt Smith. Matt had served with Marcus and told us that he was something special. He grew up in Atlanta, was a captain in the Army Special

Forces (Green Berets) and a combat veteran—and had no experience in philanthropy. But he was a veteran who really knew the issues. We took a big chance, and he turned out to be a great hire.

Marcus joined us on a tour around the country to see who was doing good work in medical philanthropy that we might support. We met with the president of UCLA, and they had a program called Operation Mend that offered free plastic surgery to veterans who had been severely injured or disfigured. The surgeons donated their services, and they took care of the families during the recovery. We were impressed, but they did not seem interested in creating a national program. But Dr. Jim Kelly, who founded and directed the National Intrepid Center of Excellence (NICoE) at Walter Reed National Military Medical Center (a brain injury facility funded by philanthropist Arnold Fisher) did. The center provided cutting-edge evaluation, treatment planning, and research and education for active service members and their families. NICoE also treated complex interactions of mild traumatic brain injuries and comorbid psychological health conditions, conducted research, and provided clinical patient care.

Intrigued by what we were doing, Dr. Kelly ultimately agreed to join us in 2015 to launch the Marcus Institute for Brain Health (MIBH) on the Anschutz Campus of the

University of Colorado School of Medicine, where he was on the faculty. Service members and veterans receive free treatment, and the clinic remains self-sufficient by taking private patients, renting out high-end diagnostic equipment, and seeking research grants. The program treats hundreds of patients every year and continues to grow. It also serves as a national hub of our TBI network. The MIBH focuses on the whole patient—if the veteran has high blood pressure or diabetes, they receive treatment for that condition free of charge as well. Our real success comes from coordination; the whole network is based on the concept of sharing information and resources among funders, doctors, nonprofits, and clinicians. In January of 2020, MIBH opened a lodge on campus in a historic building on Colonels Row.

Veterans find out about the center through an informal network of "battle buddies." Retired Army 1st Sergeant Raymond W. told us how the institute impacted his life: "After retiring from twenty-one years as an Army EOD Tech (Bomb Squad), I had multiple deployments, multiple concussions, TBI, and post-traumatic symptoms. I had lost my purpose and my confidence, and my emotional state was deteriorating. I had no good answers. I was quickly losing hope. A neurologist referred me to the MIBH and that all changed. I can't begin to tell you how this amazing team of specialists changed the outlook for my future. I'm just one soldier among many that struggle with brain health, but my life will forever be changed. I can't thank the team from the MIBH enough."

MIBH became the clinical hub that collaborates with other clinics around the country. We now have centers in Atlanta (SHARE Military Initiative), New Orleans (Tulane University Center for Brain Health), Philadelphia (Veterans' Brain Institute at Thomas Jefferson University/MossRehab), Jacksonville (University of Florida Haley Brain Wellness Program), and Chapel Hill (Transforming Health and Resilience in Veterans Program at the University of North Carolina, Chapel Hill). We have three more in the pipeline in San Diego, Houston, and New York, places that have high populations of retired military personnel. Our goal is to make sure every veteran who wants treatment can get it.

Because Marcus Ruzek was a veteran and a member of the Army Reserves, he was able to participate in charities and nonprofit programs as a veteran rather than as an employee of the Marcus Foundation. That gave him a unique perspective and an opportunity to ask: "Is this worth my time? Would this help me if I were struggling?" If the answer was no, he moved on to something else. In May 2018, he joined a fellow veteran in the Warrior PATHH program at Boulder Crest, a training program founded on the science of post-traumatic growth. The experience highlighted areas related to the trauma of war that he had tucked away. In fact, another one of our employees at the Marcus Foundation later completed the program. Because of his unique background and position, Marcus started asking partner organizations a question about accountability. In each meeting, he would ask, "What do you *require* of veterans? What do you ask *them* to do in return for your support?" This was a way to see if the organization was serious about fostering independence and self-respect. Veterans were not weak, broken, or in need of rescue. They offered a lot of value, were self-sacrificing, and cared about being good citizens.

COMPREHENSIVE, COORDINATED SOLUTIONS

SHARE, MIBH, Boulder Crest—they all worked. But we keep pushing Marcus Ruzek and Jim Kelly to create a national network that will truly address the major issues facing veterans. We are not going to be satisfied until we do. Philanthropy should be empowering, not patronizing. We want veterans to know that they play a critical role in their own healing. We used our do-it-yourself philosophy that shaped Home Depot to tackle this problem, but that did not mean do it alone. Our giving to Boulder Crest; Team Red, White & Blue; the Gary Sinise Foundation;

the Stephen Siller Tunnel to Towers Foundation; Team Rubicon, the Mission Continues; and the Warrior Alliance met the criteria. Each one of these organizations has a great story, but we started to feel like our giving was scattered. As Marcus Ruzek once said to me, "We were a mile wide, but an inch deep." We were helping, but we were not having the kind of impact we expected. So we made a decision to focus on traumatic brain injuries and post-traumatic stress disorder and take a three-pronged approach—clinical interventions, immersive retreat programs, and substance abuse and addiction treatment. The decision was motivated by a big problem: There were very few comprehensive, coordinated solutions to help veterans. So we had some work to do.

In January 2019, we launched the Avalon Fund to create an integrated, national network to help veterans heal. We had been talking with Arthur Blank, and we knew he wanted to help. But "the how" turned out to be a huge surprise. In May 2019, I turned ninety, and my friends Doug Hertz and Mike Leven organized a big birthday party at the Georgia Aquarium that would raise funds for causes that are important to me: the Georgia Aquarium, SHARE, the Marcus Stroke and Neuroscience Center, and the Marcus Autism Center. Arthur was the keynote speaker, and he talked about our years together, calling me his "father, brother, and rabbi." He even joked, "We shared the same bathroom for forty years. That's longer than any of my marriages lasted." Then came the bombshell: He volunteered to donate $5 million to the SHARE initiative and another $15 million to the Avalon Fund. I couldn't believe it—I was totally surprised, and so were his own people at the Arthur M. Blank Family Foundation. He hadn't told anybody. That gift put us well on our way toward raising $200 million, and we've had Lockheed Martin, USAA, the Goldring Foundation, the Manat Foundation, the Irsay family, Pratt Industries, and the Veterans United Foundation come on board as well.

Our goal is to create more centers like SHARE, MIBH, and Boulder Crest to treat complex TBI and PTSD cases and to focus on the science of post-traumatic growth. In the next few years, our hope is that we will be treating 10,000 veterans and family members annually and serve as a model for best practices nationally. We will not rest until every veteran who suffers the invisible wounds of war has the opportunity to turn that struggle into profound strength. If we properly treat our veterans, we will heal our nation. We keep detailed data on outcomes and know that these programs work and could be scaled to help first responders and professional athletes who get injured or accident victims—anyone who needs it. Self-sufficiency is the key. We insist that each organization create a business model that can survive long after we're gone.

Solving this problem has become my life's work, and I hope it inspires you to find something you are equally passionate about. But know that there is no roadmap when you "do it yourself." When we built Home Depot or became involved with the CDC and veterans causes, we had no idea where we were going to end up, and no Harvard MBA could have helped us. We were in unchartered waters, and there was nobody to tell us what was right or wrong.

But we did have plenty of common sense, something I inherited from my mother. She taught me to look at a situation critically to really understand the issue, to trust my own judgment, but not be so stubborn that I wouldn't listen to other viewpoints and take advice. She also taught me not to sit around and wait for others to fix things. She was a poor immigrant in a country filled with opportunity and was not going to waste a single minute. Neither should you.

CHAPTER 7

DO IT YOURSELF DOES NOT MEAN DO IT ALONE

I have had some success, because I learned to build the right team. I did not hire people who thought like me. I wanted to bring in colleagues who were willing to voice their opinions. I also wanted entrepreneurs who could solve problems on their own—that's why each Home Depot store manager was empowered to be creative. We didn't want them to go rogue, but also didn't want them to call us for every little problem. They had to embrace the same do-it-yourself spirit that they were selling every day.

I have seen plenty of bad teams. I've seen dysfunctional companies, and I cannot tell you how many good pitches we turned down at the Marcus Foundation because the organization did not have the right people in place. They had weak leadership. They had an ineffective board. They had not given careful thought to how their project could be scaled or sustained. They were not able to pivot when something went wrong. Success requires that you get the right people for the right job, show that you trust them, and make sure they are in the room when you need them. I've been lucky to have a number of people help me along the way and just as many who showed me what not to do.

LUCKY BREAKS

Herbie Hubschman was my boss at Two Guys, back in the 1960s, and I perfected my do-it-yourself attitude under him. He was certifiably nuts. He never slept and was in the store all the time, trying new ways to entice customers. He had an innate sense of what customers wanted and would make unusual deals with manufacturers to ensure that they had plenty of merchandise—he once bought all the inventory from a Lionel toy train factory. I learned about selective hearing from watching him. He listened to his customers and employees and knew a good idea when he heard one, but also knew his own mind. He was a tough boss, and we shared a love for honest, straight talk. He gave me the opportunity to take chances and try new things and expected everyone that worked for him to be entrepreneurial. We never bullshitted each other, and I give him credit for giving me my biggest, luckiest break. I cut my teeth at Two Guys, and never could have started Home Depot without Herbie's mentorship.

EVEN MY UNDERWEAR WAS WET

Like Herbie, Sam Walton was a major influence in my life. He was one of the great merchants of our time, and there is no question that Walmart transformed the retail landscape in our country. I first met Sam at a retail analyst meeting, and we became fast friends. He and I used to pick a market—let's say, Miami—and travel there to visit each other's stores. We would start at Home Depot, and he would walk the whole store with me, pointing out what he thought we could do better. Then I did the same for him at Walmart. We weren't Mr. Walton and Mr. Marcus, the CEOs, we were just two retailers trying to help each other. He pointed out our inadequate computer systems and sold me on his concept of "everyday low prices," arguing that it was more efficient and profitable than running constant sales. His approach helped us build a larger customer base, encouraging people to shop us every day instead of chasing the promise of some future sale. It took us awhile to make this change, but our willingness to listen to alternative viewpoints and take constructive advice became baked into our leadership. Sam's advice led us to develop a new slogan: "Home Depot: Where Low Prices Are Just the Beginning."

I liked visiting Sam in Bentonville, Arkansas, but hated traveling with him in the summer because his old red truck didn't have air-conditioning. On my first trip, he insisted on driving us to lunch. I was soaking wet by the time we got there. Even my underwear was wet. I kept saying, "Sam, what is wrong with you? Go see a mechanic." That first trip I was expecting a nice lunch. But there I was trying to dry my underwear sitting in a crappy restaurant in the middle of Arkansas.

Sam never fixed that AC, and from that point on, every time I visited Arkansas, he took me to the same restaurant. It seemed to be a source of pride. He must have been a great guy because I would not have done that with anybody else. Sam was also legendary for staying at the cheapest hotels, and making his executives sleep four to a room. He was frugal, just like his customers. I think that's what made him successful.

Each year David Glass, who became president and chief operating officer at Walmart in 1984, and Sam had a contest. Each man selected a product that would be featured prominently in the store (what they called a value producing item, or VPI). They often asked me to referee between the two of them. In this particular year, Sam brought me to a warehouse to see a huge pile of individually wrapped food items. I couldn't really tell what they were—but I grabbed one and took a bite, spit it out, and yelled, "What is this crap?"

It was a Moon Pie, a marshmallow sandwich treat invented in 1917 by a traveling salesman. I thought it was terrible and was sure it would never sell, so I voted for David's product, though now I can't even remember what it was. Turns out I was wrong—Walmart customers went wild for Moon Pies. The company struggled like crazy to keep up with demand. Sam had great instincts, and what did I know about pies? The only thing I never understood about him was that he was not very interested in philanthropy outside of his hometown. I tried to get him involved in the City of Hope, but he only wanted to work with charities that directly helped Walmart. He built a hospital in Bentonville so he could hire people and take care of them.

Sam and I were close friends until the day he died in 1992 at the age of seventy-four. I was in London at a retail analyst meeting when I received a call from the vice chairman of Walmart. He asked me to stand in for him, which was unusual. He was not able to get there because Sam was on his last leg, and he had all these analysts counting on him. He swore me to secrecy, so I went to the meeting and talked about how Walmart had influenced Home Depot. That night I received a call from Sam's biographer, and he said, "I'm sorry to call so late, but Sam's in and out of consciousness, and I'm supposed to get a quote from you for the book. He wakes up, asks if I got in touch with you and Sol Price, then falls back into the coma. Please give me something." So I did, and within the week Sam died. About six months later, I ran into the author, and he told me that Sam kept asking over and over again, "Did you get a quote from Bernie and Sol?" Once the biographer said yes, Sam seemed satisfied and never regained consciousness. I'll never know for sure if that's true, but he was a great friend and mentor who had terrible taste in trucks and snack food.

ENTRUST THE NATION

I have been lucky to have met so many brilliant people in my life—presidents and prime ministers, leading doctors and scientists who have cured and pioneered treatments for disease, entrepreneurs who have helped make the American Dream possible for millions of people—but the most impressive person I ever met was George Shultz. A full accounting of his résumé would fill this entire chapter, but in brief:

Born in 1920, George helped shape American economic and foreign policy for much of the second half of the twentieth century. A World War II veteran, he received a doctorate from MIT in industrial economics and joined the faculty. In 1957, he moved to the University of Chicago, became dean of their graduate school of business, and was a senior staff economist with Dwight D. Eisenhower's Council of Economic Advisers. He was president of the Bechtel Group before serving as secretary of labor under Richard Nixon and secretary of state under Ronald Reagan. In 1989, he was given the Presidential Medal of Freedom and became a fellow at the Hoover Institution at Stanford University. Henry Kissinger once said in his diary, "If I could choose one American to whom I would entrust the nation's fate in a crisis, it would be George Shultz." Not bad for a kid who grew up in Englewood, New Jersey.

George had worked hard in the Middle East, resolving the Lebanese civil war and working to bring Israel and the Palestinians to the negotiating table. As secretary of state, he also arranged the release of Russian Jews, and built a strong relationship with Mikhail Gorbachev. Shultz's deep commitment to Israel was personal. While a professor at the University of Chicago in the 1960s, he had an honors student in economics, Joseph Levy, who voluntarily enlisted in the IDF in 1967 to serve in the Six-Day War against Egypt and Syria. George could not understand why he would willingly interrupt his education and asked, "How can a young man with all this ambition give it all up for his country?" That's exactly what Joseph did, and he was killed in action liberating Jerusalem. George used to say that Joseph taught him three things about Israel: "There is a wonderful individual quality to its people, they have an instinctive patriotism, and they live in a lousy neighborhood." Joseph's death deeply impacted George. He teared up any time he told the story, and his support for the country was rooted in this deep connection.

When George's six-year term as secretary of state came to an end in January 1989, he was still active and engaged in the region. That's how we came to work together building the Israel Democracy Institute (IDI). I learned so much from George. I think he was the only person who ever intimidated me. Jay Kaiman and I used to go to his house, and he and his wife, Charlotte, would host huge dinners that felt like State Department retreats with brilliant minds from around the world. The conversations would go deep into the night, and the next morning George would cook me breakfast—sometimes pancakes or French toast. The two of us could talk for hours about all kinds of things. Looking back now, I see that those breakfasts were instrumental to my life. George was the most honorable man I ever met, and though you would never know it, he taught me a great deal about diplomacy, especially about getting all the facts before making a decision. George may have been the only person who could actually get me to keep my mouth shut.

LIEUTENANT DAN

My respect for George is matched by my affection for Gary Sinise. You probably know him best from his iconic role as Lieutenant Dan Taylor in the 1994 film *Forrest Gump*. Not long after the movie came out, the Disabled American Veterans organization invited him to their national convention to give him an award. There were more than 2,000 disabled veterans in the audience, and it was then that he realized how much his character had resonated with servicemen and women. Gary used to talk about how World War II and Vietnam veterans in his family affected his need to serve. After September 11, he worked to balance his acting career, with *Criminal Minds* and *CSI: NY*, with foundation work and visiting troops in war zones through the USO. He even started the Lt. Dan

Band and still plays at bases all over the world. In 2011, he started the Gary Sinise Foundation and not long after approached the Marcus Foundation about helping to build specially equipped houses for veterans without limbs.

Lots of charities provide housing assistance, but few are specifically designed to address limitations born of these injuries. Toilets, showers, cabinets, and appliances are often inaccessible. Doors often do not accommodate wheelchairs. I knew something about home building and home improvement, so this was close to my heart. We partnered with Gary and the Stephen Siller Tunnel to Towers Foundation. We started out funding the construction on our own, but soon realized that we were stronger together, and leveraged the work of the two foundations to help serve this often-forgotten group. The homes cost about $700,000, the VA contributes roughly ten percent, the rest comes from donations. It is a rare thing to truly solve a problem, but in this case we did, and Gary became a dear friend. I put him in a category of people whom I consider angels. He sacrificed a lucrative Hollywood career to spend all his time and energy trying to make life easier for the men and women who serve our nation. He is the very embodiment of "do it yourself." He saw a problem and was determined to fix it. Every day, he serves.

I've been lucky to have the right people helping and guiding me, and you often don't know how much they have helped until they are gone. But I also discovered that you learn just as much from the bastards in your life.

THREE KINDS OF BOSSES

Harvey Mackay interviewed me for his 2004 book, *We Got Fired! . . . And It's the Best Thing That Ever Happened to Us*, where he also tells the stories of Billie Jean King, Michael Bloomberg, Lou Holtz, and others who found that getting the ax changed the trajectory of their lives. Being fired by Sandy Sigoloff not only motivated Arthur Blank and me to start Home Depot, it helped us articulate our values. Sandy was everything a boss should not be—hotheaded, mercurial, and vengeful. He actually got pleasure out of treating people badly. We used to have terrible fights; one in particular stands out to me even today. Daylin, the parent company of Handy Dan, was in bankruptcy and we found that a lot of vendors would not ship to us. Handy Dan was an independent company, but they were still nervous. So I spent a lot of time with our bankers and one guy in particular who invested a lot in Handy Dan. He was a great guy, and I kept him up to date on everything. Sandy found out and told me I should treat all the bankers like idiots because they don't know what they are doing. I disagreed and kept building the kinds of relationships that I had always built. This just gave Sandy one more thing to hate about me. But he helped me see that there were three kinds of bosses: The first are hardworking and honest, flexible, and bright. The second fake their way through and rise to the level of their incompetence. Then, there were people like Sandy, who were vicious and took special pleasure in stepping over people's bodies. They were the bullies. Arthur and I were determined to be the first kind of boss, never hire the second, and steer clear of the third.

THE CADILLAC

When Arthur Blank, Ken Langone, and I started Home Depot, we needed investors. You can't just start a business out of thin air—and we did not have the kind of capital it would have taken to bring our vision to market. This was no mom-and-pop enterprise. This would be big, and we needed money fast. We had been trying for a while, only to end up at another dead end. Now, we were starting to feel desperate. While we were still trying to start the company, Ken called Arthur and me and said, "I got $2 million from Ross Perot." I couldn't believe it. The founder of Electronic Data Systems (EDS) was going to help make our dreams come true. Who cared that we had to give him seventy percent of the company in exchange for a two-million-dollar cash infusion? If we had done the deal, Ross's initial investment would be worth nearly $100 billion today.

But the whole deal fell apart over my car. I drove a used Cadillac, nothing fancy, but I loved it. Ross objected. He expected his executives to drive Chevrolets and would not even consider any other option. While listening to his explanation and even though he tried to reassure me that I would run the company, it suddenly became clear that this was a bad deal for both of us. The issue over the car, which might have seemed insignificant, showed me that Ross did not share our values, and we did not share his. We were so anxious to secure start-up capital that we had not asked the right questions nor done our due diligence. If Ross cared about what kind of car I drove, what else would he try to micromanage? If we gave up a controlling interest in the company, we would have spent the rest of our careers under his thumb. I had just left one job where I worked with a son of a bitch, and I was not about to step into another bad situation. Ross was smart as hell, was a great patriot, and had lots of good qualities, but he would have been a terrible partner for us. So we walked away.

THE WRONG TOOLBOX

When I left Home Depot, Arthur Blank took over for a few years, then the board hired Robert Nardelli in late December 2000 after he was passed up for the senior job at General Electric (GE). As the former president and chief executive officer of GE Power Systems, he was brought on as Home Depot's president and chief executive, then added the chairman's title. He was good friends with Ken Langone, and we really thought he was the right person for the job. I was supportive of the hire and took Jack Welch's advice and moved off the scene.

Wall Street had high hopes for Nardelli. We all believed he would be like King Midas, that everything he touched would turn to gold. Instead, he tarnished everything. He was a disrupter—but of the wrong things. Home Depot's culture was the key to our success. Associates and customers alike were loyal—but Nardelli never seemed to understand that. He centralized some divisions, modernized stores and their technology, and closed the Home Depot Expo Design Centers. Those were not bad decisions, but he got into trouble when he fired longtime Home Depot executives, brought in new management from GE, and did not give associates the same opportunities for advancement. It was like he was trying to erase everything that made Home Depot great.

About a year after I stepped down as CEO, I was in a store on a Monday morning. I was stunned by how neat and organized it was. Usually, after a busy weekend, there would be lumber everywhere. I found the manager and asked what was happening. He explained, "We don't sell much lumber anymore because we raised our prices." I called a dozen other stores and got the same story. Lumber was our bread and butter, so I set up a meeting with Nardelli to discuss the issue. I was still the chairman and felt like it was my responsibility to understand what was going on. Nardelli pulled out spreadsheet after spreadsheet to show how much lumber we were selling, but it was all bullshit. I trusted the managers. We had a shareholders' meeting in Chicago, so I went a few days early and took a legal pad into every competitor within a thirty-mile radius to compare prices on our most popular items—lumber, hardware, electrical and plumbing supplies, and paint. I went to the meeting with a spreadsheet of my own, which showed that across the board we were charging the highest prices of anyone and were losing sales to our competitors. Instead of using the data to address the problem, Nardelli said, "I'll fix this, and do me a favor and stay out of my stores." I realized that it was time for me to go. When I became chairman, I agreed to move my office down to the twenty-first floor and stay for three years. After that meeting in Chicago, I packed my things and left. I knew Nardelli was never going to take advice from me or Arthur because he removed all of our pictures from the headquarters.

Nardelli GE-ized the company, and it didn't work. He brought the wrong toolbox, and we lost a ton of talent. Associates became faceless numbers, and he crushed the entrepreneurial spirit that made people "bleed orange." He brought in more part-timers, diminishing our customer service. He thought he could replace people with technology. He overfocused on processes and cost cutting and completely ignored what made Home Depot great. Nardelli also instilled a culture of fear. He did very little to build connections to the city's philanthropic efforts and was not involved in top civic organizations.

But what really sunk his ship was the now infamous May 2006 shareholders' meeting in Wilmington, Delaware. He refused to allow shareholders to ask questions outside of a strict one-minute time slot and ended the meeting after thirty minutes. One attendee, Richard Ferlauto, complained about CEO pay, equating it to a canary in a coal mine. He went on to lambast Nardelli: "Here at the Home Depot, I'm afraid that canary has died. While you have been handsomely compensated, the stock price has languished . . . You've got a good deal. As a long-term investor, I want you to earn your keep, but we want to see pay-for-performance." They had plenty of reason to be concerned. Nardelli was given an enormous compensation package—more than $131 million from 2000 to 2006—as our stock dropped nine percent. Our nearest competitor, Lowe's, saw its shares skyrocket by 185 percent. Nardelli would only last seven more months because the board did not renew his contract. The bad news was that he walked away with $210 million—money that could have been better spent on training, building new stores, or on anything else but lining his pockets.

The day the board hired Frank Blake to replace Nardelli, Frank called me in a panic. "Bernie, I have to meet with you right away. They just made me CEO, and I'm not sure I can do it." Frank had been an executive vice president since 2002, and we spent a whole Sunday together in Florida talking about the company and its future. I gave him an earful, and he took pages of notes. A month later, he called again, and we continued the conversation. Frank had also worked at GE, but unlike Nardelli, he embraced the original Home Depot culture and understood that his role as the new CEO was to stabilize things. He returned the company to what we envisioned and did so much more. He was a rock star and saved the company.

Bob Nardelli was there for six years and did a lot of damage. I partly blame myself because I helped hire him. But it is not uncommon for a leader to be successful in one environment and flop in another. Frank lived Home Depot values; Craig Menear, who started as a buyer while I was still CEO, did the same thing until his retirement in 2022. Ted Decker, who joined Home Depot in 2000, picked up the baton as CEO in March 2022. I feel pretty lucky that, except for Nardelli, our successive leaders have been strong evangelists for our culture—Arthur, Frank, Craig, and Ted.

In all my years, I learned another powerful lesson: You will make some bad calls. No matter how hard you try, your judgment is going to fail you sometimes. We thought Nardelli was a good choice but turned out to be dead wrong. It's easy to be wowed by a résumé or long list of accomplishments, but being a good fit is far more important. If you keep toxic or unproductive associates, managers, or executives, your business will suffer in the long run.

I remember one comptroller at Daylin. He was a nice guy, but a terrible CFO. They wanted to fire him, but I stepped in and stopped it because of my affection for him. Later on, he would be instrumental in getting *me* fired and leading the lawsuit against me. The lesson? Don't let personal feelings override your good business sense. If you have people around you that don't share your values or understand your vision, they will become a liability, and it's best to let them go before they become even more dangerous.

Plenty of people have helped me along the way. I believed in our vision but knew it would never come to fruition if we couldn't get others to buy into it. The people who worked for Home Depot really loved the company, and they felt respected and heard. We gave people freedom to make decisions in the stores and take responsibility for them. In that way, they became committed not only to the store but to the whole Home Depot family. They are the backbone of this company and illustrate that the American Dream is still alive and well.

I love the story of one associate, whose mother-in-law cut a hiring advertisement out of the newspaper and gave it to him. He was an ex-Marine looking for a new job. He never had a chance to go to college but started as an hourly employee and was given plenty of opportunity at Home Depot. He eventually became a division head, overseeing nine hundred stores and $20 billion a year.

Ann-Marie Campbell tells a similar story. A native of Jamaica, she started as a cashier in one of our South Florida stores. I hated to see long lines at the register, and one day, I was in her store and saw a huge line but no cashier.

I grabbed the manager and asked, "What's going on?"

"Oh, that's Ann-Marie's register. She is out selling again."

It turned out that when someone came through her line with a can of paint, she asked if they had brushes, primer, tape, paint thinner, and drop cloths. If not, she walked them to that aisle to help them find what they needed. My response was "Put her on the sales floor!" They did, and she used the lessons she learned in retail from her grandmother in Jamaica who owned a small furniture store. No surprise that she moved up the ranks. Today she is the executive vice president for U.S. stores and international operations. She oversees 2,317 stores and 500,000 associates, and manages supply chain, merchandising, sourcing, and strategy for Home Depot Canada and Mexico. While working for us, she earned her business bachelor's degree and MBA at Georgia State University. Her story shows that hard work, common sense, and dedication can take you wherever you want to go. That's why I love this company.

WHAT HAPPENS WHEN YOU'RE THE BASTARD?

I learned early on at Home Depot that you can't go it alone. When we started the company, I had a lot of retail experience, and I was pretty confident in my decision-making. One day, I was meeting with Arthur Blank, Pat Farrah, and Ron Brill, and they were all three challenging me on something. I can't even remember what the issue was, but we were having a pretty heated discussion.

Exasperated by their endless stream of questions, I finally got fed up and said, "This is bullshit. I'm CEO, and I'm making this decision." All their faces dropped as they slinked out of the room.

That night, I woke up at four o'clock in the morning in a panic. All I could think was, "Holy shit. My life is on the line. I'm fifty, and if this goes down the drain, where do I go? These are bright people. Why did I just discount what they said? Why didn't I listen?" I was so sure of myself that I couldn't even hear a dissenting opinion.

The next day, I called them into my office. They were reluctant to come in because they were all still pissed at me. I sat them down and said, "Look guys. I can't build this by myself. If I've learned one thing it's that I have to respect your judgment and opinions and listen more carefully."

I had become the kind of boss that we all hated. Once, in pharmacy school, somebody had told me, "If your mouth is open, your jawbone blocks your ears." I thought of that quote: Damnit, that was me! They were shocked when I said, "I want you to just go through this issue and tell me again why you think I was wrong." I listened and really tried to understand what they were saying. I considered it and was not trying to formulate a rebuttal. I really wanted to hear why all three of them thought I was wrong. I don't even remember what we were discussing or what we decided to do, but I do remember from that day forward I began to listen more carefully and let go of the urge to fight for my own way of doing things. There are other bright people in this world, and when you really respect their opinions, you have to listen to what they have to say.

We were in such a hurry to get Home Depot off the ground that I forgot this critical lesson—you never know who will give you the next bright idea. It might be from a first-time customer, a contractor, or a kid who came in with their parents. I walked through stores and slowed down to listen to customers and associates, and this new approach spilled over into my personal life. I was so busy building the business that I don't think I was a very good husband or friend—so I started to really listen to Billi and our dear friends. It was like a reawakening. I'm not the smartest person in the world—and even if you are, there are always people out there you can learn from. The art of listening is just that—an art. Shut down your own voice and hear what the other person is saying. That doesn't mean you agree with them or even that they are right. It just means you need to hear them out. Close your mouth, stop trying to plan your response, and maybe you will hear something important. Who knows? Maybe it will turn into a million-dollar solution.

I'm telling you, this new approach really started to

make a difference. One day, I was walking a store, talking to some of the associates, and watching a team working in operations. They were putting all this merchandise on the shelves, and we started talking.

"How long does this take you?" I wondered

One of the newer associates answered, "Almost half a day. Why don't we just put each item in a case and have the manufacturer set the cases on the shelf? That would save time and money."

I talked to Pat Farrah, and he went back to the manufacturer who agreed to cut the tops off the boxes for items sold in bulk so they could be easily placed on the floor or on shelves and customers could grab what they needed. That idea saved us millions of dollars in operational costs, and the manufacturer sold the new packaging to our competitors, who also saved money. A brilliant idea came from a simple suggestion from a teenager who had been there less than ninety days. That is listening. Do it because it will keep you from being the bastard, too.

CHAPTER 8

DON'T LEAVE YOUR BUSINESS SENSE AT THE DOOR

Two concepts in the Jewish tradition—*tikkun olam* (repair the world) and *tzedakah* (giving to others)—are essential to understanding my story. I have worked hard in my life, but I have also been very lucky. I believe that we all have a responsibility to make the world a better place, to help those who are vulnerable and whose families are suffering. I have focused my philanthropy on causes that share this vision and commitment. But I also want to use what I learned in business to ensure that my investment creates momentum and is sustainable. We have donated more than $2 billion over thirty years to more than five hundred organizations through the Marcus Foundation. With each one, we try to answer four questions before deciding whether to commit: What are the deliverables? How will we measure success? How capable is leadership? What is the organization's plan for self-sufficiency and sustainability? Charity is no different from business: The bottom line matters.

We do not just want to give money. We want to create, support, and sustain programs and organizations that cure diseases, promote free enterprise, and change people's lives. We want to help redefine the metrics that philanthropists use to distribute their wealth. Most grantees come to the Marcus Foundation and want to do good for a specific number of people over a specific amount of time to show specific results. That is a noble cause, but often shortsighted. We approach each ask as a challenge and, in conversation with the partner, try to create an innovative solution that will have a big impact. If we can come to an agreement, then we will provide the necessary resources to help them reach the finish line. It is not unusual for someone to come to the Marcus Foundation with a good, but not fully formed, idea and ask for $50,000. After a few conversations, they might walk out with $500,000 because they were willing to step back and think about how their work might be leveraged into a more sustainable solution. If you take $100 and leverage it to $1,000 by getting ten friends to join you—that's good business. You don't have to be rich to make a difference—you just have to get involved. If I had a motto, it would be: Do the most good with the best people to have the biggest impact.

LET'S DO GOOD THINGS

The return on your investment should be measured by metrics. How many lives have been saved? Did the research you funded discover a drug to help cure a specific disease? Did your new educational program support underserved children? You see a need, and it's your job to figure out a solution. Whether you give big or small, you can make a difference. When we received the phone call from my accountant that we were billionaires, I went to my wife, Billi, and said, "We can buy anything we want—or we can change the world. What do you want to do?" Quickly, Billi said, "Let's do good things." And we created the Marcus Foundation for that sole purpose.

Americans at every economic level are generous donors to charity—be it a school, church, or nonprofit. It's not only the Warren Buffetts of the world that give, and I have found that entrepreneurs who built something from scratch often approach philanthropy from a hands-on perspective. I did not invent the concept of entrepreneurial philanthropy, but I do practice it. This is what that looks like.

Philo Alto wrote in the *Stanford Social Innovation Review* that effective giving often requires six steps. The first step is to study the issue. Writing a check is easy, but you need to invest time in understanding what the nonprofit or charity is trying to do before you invest. You might be asked by a friend or family member who is involved in the cause to help, but before you do so, do some homework. The second step is to determine how best to get involved. Do you want to attend a few meetings or be part of a planning team? Third, you have to decide what Alto calls "the horizon of impact." Are you trying to solve a short-term issue—like hurricane relief—or are you trying to re-shape how a disease is studied and treated? The next issue is to assess if there is a tipping point—is there a way that your support can "trigger a massive impact." We found this with the autism center. There was very little care or treatment available to families when we started, and our work totally changed that reality. Fifth, you have to de-cide what resources to deploy—how much will you give and in what way? Do you give seed money and encour-age the nonprofit to look for matching funds? Do you give money over three years and encourage them to look for sustainable solutions? Finally, you need a way to track your progress. Did your gift help meet the organization's goals, or did it fall short? Do you need to recalibrate, and is the project worth continuing to support? All of these steps are just another way of saying: Put the same kind of energy that made you successful in your business into your philanthropy.

PUT ON YOUR SEAT BELT

I have sat on a lot of charitable boards, and most of them are undisciplined, badly managed, or completely ineffective. Sometimes all three! It is astonishing to see all these successful people serving without accomplishing much. It is as if everything they learned in business just flew out the window. I remember one board that I won't name to keep from embarrassing anyone. But it was a well-known charity that was doing important work, and the Marcus Foundation was a major funder. I knew the chairman, and we talked a lot about the problems they were having. It became pretty clear that they had a weak board—members were not engaged, and it was hard to get anybody to commit to anything—and his leadership was a big part of the problem. After about a year and a half, the chairman recommended replacing the entire board—and resigning to show how serious he was. He was savvy enough to realize that he was the weak link. Almost overnight, they were changed. They recruited a strong chair and brought on board members that had unique skills and were ready to get their hands dirty. They went from a two on a scale of ten to a seven in six months. Today, they are highly effective. As a funder, our job is not to change an organization, but we do step away when we see significant problems that prevent them from achieving their mission.

If I were advising a nonprofit, I'd tell them to put Kenny Langone on their board. He serves on mine. Ken was a well-known investor who helped us build Home Depot. He is a terrific businessman, major philanthropist, and one of my closest friends. But if you invite him to sit on your board, you better put on your seat belt because it's going to be a wild ride.

Ken doesn't come for the free lunch. He talks to everyone inside and outside your organization. He meets with financial people, marketing people, HR, fundraisers, clients, trade associations, and your competitors. He brings the same critical eye to your board that he used with us at Home Depot. He is going to point out your weaknesses, problems with your balance sheets, your blind spots, and when you are straying from your core business or mission. He is an active board member who is careful not to micromanage. He only signs on to things that he cares deeply about and feels his skills and experience can make better. His work at New York University (NYU) is a great example.

Ken donated $10 million to NYU's part-time MBA program and joined the medical school as chairman of the board in 1999. He did more than just chair the board—he got involved. For more than a decade he worked closely with NYU dean Robert Grossman, and they strategized about what would have the biggest impact. Ken grew up the son of Italian immigrants, a plumber and a cafeteria worker, who lived paycheck to paycheck. He dug ditches for the Long Island Expressway to pay the tuition for his degree in economics from Bucknell University in Pennsylvania. Ken thought he understood the importance of an affordable education—until a meeting with a pediatrician changed his whole outlook. She was thirty years out of medical school, was still saddled with a ton of debt, and was afraid she was not going to be able to help her son go to college. Inspired by her story, Ken donated $200 million and helped raise $350 million more to pay the tuition for every NYU medical student. That translates to about $200,000 per student, and his goal is to encourage the recipients of the tuition reimbursement to go on to help somebody else. Pay it forward. In 2008, the medical center was renamed NYU Langone Health to honor Ken's contributions.

At Home Depot, we insisted that board members visit

stores and meet with managers, associates, and customers. We wanted them to ask tough questions: What works well? What issues are causing you the most problems? What frustrates customers the most? How do your systems operate? What happens when they fail? Why would you shop at our competitor? The result was that board members came to meetings energized to share what they learned. If somebody did not have time to do that legwork, we asked them to leave the board. Ken has served on the board at the Marcus Foundation since it started, and he is a world-class pain in the ass—questioning everything and making his opinions known. In other words, we appreciate every minute of it.

OVERGIVE AND UNDERACHIEVE

I learned the hard way that philanthropy, just like your business, needs to be focused and strategic. In 2002, soon after I left Home Depot, I was able to commit myself to giving full time. The Marcus Foundation had been up and running since 1989, and, at first, we used a "buckshot approach." We fired money here and there at whatever piqued our interest that week. I felt like we helped fix some small problems but were not making a measurable difference. What could we do differently?

You may not understand how hard it is to manage a foundation. Every day, well-meaning people come to us with good causes. Unless you discipline yourself and focus on specific areas where you can have an impact, you will "overgive and underachieve," as my friend Mike Leven often says. So, after working for several years with Curtis Meadows, an experienced consultant, we decided to narrow the field to those things that we cared deeply about and that needed support. Curtis had run the Meadows Foundation and offered us a lot of practical advice, notably about sticking to a relatively narrow range of areas where we could have a big impact. I always say he helped us go from being amateurs to the big leagues.

He helped us see the advantage of giving while you live. Some philanthropists create their foundations to last in perpetuity, like the Ford Foundation or the Rockefeller Foundation. But I want to sunset mine within twenty years of my death. When I signed the Giving Pledge in 2010, I wrote about my intention to Warren Buffett: "It has always been my belief that leaving enormous wealth for our children does nothing to stimulate their ability to make it on their own. I, too, believe that all our efforts in creating the wealth that we have would give us a great deal more joy if we were to disperse as much of it as we can within our lifetimes." There was good reason to do so. Martin Wooster's book *How Great Philanthropists*

Failed and How You Can Succeed at Protecting Your Legacy documents how Henry Ford, J. Howard Pew, Andrew Carnegie, and John D. MacArthur left few instructions or restrictions on how the funds should be spent. I saw this firsthand with other foundations that had been set up by friends or colleagues. Who knows what my successors might do with the money? That's just too big a risk to take.

My wife, Billi, and I have adult children, and two of them sit on the foundation's board. In addition, they have their own foundation, so I know that good work will continue for many years. Upon my death, ninety percent of my remaining assets will go to the Marcus Foundation. Then the clock starts ticking. They have twenty years to give it all away. This will help ensure that my assets go to causes that I personally support and that they will be spent wisely by people who know my intentions. If you don't sunset, you're crazy. One of the best parts of giving is seeing how lives are changed. There is so much joy in helping somebody, and how am I going to do that from a coffin?

FOCUS ON FIVE

We do not spend much time promoting the Marcus Foundation. You won't find a splashy website, logo, or slick brochures. We have a small staff that stays in close contact with our grantees, meeting with them regularly and constantly evaluating the deliverables and their effectiveness. Our giving is about impact, not aggrandizement. The best things in my life have come from having the right team. At Home Depot, I was lucky to work with Arthur Blank, Ron Brill, Pat Farrah, and Ken Langone. At the foundation, I have Jay Kaiman. For its first several years, the foundation was a pretty informal affair and Rick Slagle, my right-hand man, oversaw our giving. He was followed by my good friend Mike Leven, who took the helm when he finished his work at Microtel and before I tapped him to become interim CEO at the Georgia Aquarium. That's where Jay came in.

Jay started his career in his family's metal business in Pensacola, Florida, and then went on to work with the United Way. He then moved to Atlanta to oversee the Anti-Defamation League's Southeast Office. We regularly donated to the ADL, but I came to know Jay when I declined his invitation. He came to meet with me in 1996 about being the honoree for the ADL's Abe Goldstein Human Relations Award. I told him that I only accept one award a year and was booked up for the next two. Not to be deterred, he said, "Okay, we'll put you down for 1998."

Jay and I saw each other occasionally at events during

the next few years, and one day he came to propose a new grant. The Marcus Foundation board was much smaller then—only me, Billi, Ken, and a few others—and we had been listening to long-winded PowerPoint pitches all day. We were wiped out. Jay was the last presenter, and instead of giving us a dog-and-pony show with splashy graphics, he just stood up and told a compelling story of why the grant was needed and how it would impact the community. I don't think he even brought in a computer or notepad. Jay got the grant, and we eventually hired him as a program manager. He had the perfect blend of experience with business and nonprofits and had an uncanny ability get to the heart of an issue. We saw his leadership potential right away.

Jay understood our mission from the first day and took the helm in 2008. He appreciated the culture at Home Depot and knew our ability to have an impact was because of the success of the company and its culture. What makes him particularly effective is his belief about developing relationships. It is very stressful to come to a foundation to ask for money, and Jay insists that we give every potential grantee a full hour to make their presentation. We can't fund everything, so we try to be kind and helpful when we say no—making suggestions and inviting them to return with a revised proposal. We know it can be disappointing, but we never want someone to feel that they have not been treated with respect. We are not like a lot of foundations that have dozens of employees and see grantees as faceless numbers in an annual report. That would betray everything we care about.

More than anybody, Jay sees that our support for Jewish causes, medicine, youth, free enterprise, and community can really make a difference. Each area represents a part of my personal story, and most of our grants touch on multiple themes. About thirty percent of our giving is dedicated to Jewish causes, such as the Israel Democracy Institute (IDI) that I talked about in the prologue to this book. We are also the lead donor for Magen David Adom (MDA), Israel's ambulance, blood service, and disaster relief organization. In 2016, we gave $25 million, and in 2020, an additional $10 million to build its new six-story center. Prior to this grant, MDA's central blood bank was vulnerable to attack. When threatened, the blood center staff would quickly move blood-processing operations and heavy equipment down to a cramped bomb shelter in the basement of the building. This was simply unsustainable, so we helped them build an underground facility. It opened in the spring of 2020. For the first time since Israel's founding in 1948, the blood supply is safe to use for all its eight million citizens and hundreds of thousands of visitors each year, regardless of their religious or political affiliation. The facility also trains staff, conducts research, handles crises, and provides emergency services nationwide. If something happens, they have trained personnel who can be on-site within three minutes. I am proud of being Jewish and am concerned about Jewry in the U.S. and abroad, as we see antisemitism lift its ugly head again and again.

Interest in medical philanthropy came from my early desire to be a doctor, and we support many different institutions and research initiatives, but one in particular stands out. Grady Hospital is Atlanta's only nationally designated trauma center, the largest public hospital–based health system in the Southeast, and the fifth-largest in the nation. It serves close to a half million patients a year, has over 5,000 doctors, nurses, and staff members, provides free care to the uninsured, and, simply put, is a lifeline for the region. If I had grown up in Atlanta, my family would have gone to Grady. Shutting it down—a possibility that was openly discussed—would be like closing Hartsfield-Jackson Airport. For years, it was plagued by corruption—staff took huge salaries and did not show up to work. Hospital facilities were seriously outdated, and they were near financial ruin with $60 million in debt. The decision to save Grady came in 2007 when Pete Correll (former CEO of Georgia-Pacific) and Tom Bell (former CEO of Cousins Properties) sat down for drinks to talk about the hospital's fate. Determined to turn things around, they met with Sam Williams (then president of the Metro Atlanta Chamber of Commerce), and he helped form a seventeen-member Greater Grady Task Force. Even a cursory review revealed that Grady was being managed by unqualified board members and there was no real financial oversight. Morale was so low that the task force suggested that a nonprofit corporation take over the operations. The decision was so controversial that Pete and his wife received death threats. But they prevailed, and the hospital was transferred to the Grady Memorial Hospital Corporation. Though a bold move, it was an important stabilization effort they hoped would give the philanthropic community confidence. That is exactly what happened.

The Woodruff Foundation donated $200 million to Grady, and Kaiser Permanente pledged $5 million. We gave $20 million in 2009 to build the Marcus Stroke and Neuroscience Center and overhaul the emergency center. I never feel compelled to put my name on things unless it directly helps the cause. In this case, it made a huge difference. Grady was suffering from a crisis of confidence, and these major gifts gave them a much-needed boost. We were not satisfied to just build a stroke center or renovate the trauma center—we wanted both to be the best in the nation. We gave a second $30 million gift to build the Marcus Trauma Center and expand the stroke center, bringing the brightest minds to Atlanta to transform the way strokes are treated. That led to us being named a Comprehensive Stroke Center in 2013. In 2018, we gave additional $15 million to create a stroke network with the goal of extending Grady's expertise to doctors throughout the nation. We knew we were successful when patients with private insurance who used to go to Emory or Piedmont Hospital started coming to Grady for emergency and stroke care. We also saw medical school students from around the country list Grady as their first choice for residencies. We did not just want to save Grady. That's not good business. We wanted to make Grady sustainable. It had to be more than a great hospital. We needed it to be a great hospital that delivered excellent care all while continuing to grow, innovate, and turn a profit. Atlanta can't live without Grady, and we are proud to have been part of its transformation.

Our third area of giving involves youth, especially those underserved and with special needs. I'm very concerned about education, which is how I came to befriend the Cuban-American rapper Armando Pérez, who you probably know as Pitbull. Steven Hantler, who directs policy initiatives for me, visited his innovative charter school, the Sports Leadership and Management Academy (SLAM!), in Miami and thought I might want to meet him. You can read about the story in the foreword, but we became fast friends and even taught a few classes together and did a podcast called "From Negative to Positive." I was surprised to learn how much we had in common—we both grew up poor with the odds stacked against us. But he cared deeply about his community and wanted to give students a better chance. His work solidified our interest in charter schools, and we have helped the Georgia Charter Schools Association with their operations and strategic planning, and supported KIPP Charter Schools. This is just one of a dozen areas where we help youth. I was lucky to get a great public school education and believe we owe that to every kid.

Several of our giving areas overlap, which is often the case for our community work. I love the story of Camp Twin Lakes, which taps into our interest in youth, community, autism, and veterans. My friend Doug Hertz, whose family founded United Distributors in Atlanta, came to me with an idea he conceived when he was taking a class at Leadership Atlanta in 1990. A lot of kids go to summer camp—but few people think about kids who have special needs or complex medical conditions. That changed in 1993 when Doug started Camp Twin Lakes. Pete Correll, who helped save Grady Hospital, donated the land, and his daughter, Elizabeth Richards, led the board for years. The camp, which now has sites in Winder and Rutledge, Georgia, serves 10,000 campers annually and provides scholarships so no child is turned away because they can't afford it. The Marcus Foundation has given millions of dollars over the years. This is a great project, and they have also started weekend retreats for active and retired service members and their families. This is just the kind of place our community needs.

Free enterprise is our final giving area. The Home Depot is a Cinderella story, and I feel lucky to have been born in this country. I want to see that same success for other small businesses, from restaurants, barbershops, cleaners, and medical offices to service and manufacturing companies with fewer than a thousand employees—these are all small businesses. There are 31.7 million of them in the United States and they employ nearly half of the workforce. They are the backbone of our economy. So, at the urging of my good friend Steve Hantler, we started the Job Creators Network (JCN) in 2011. In our early years, more businesses were closing than opening. I got a team together, and we took surveys of small businesses to find out what they needed, where we could help. People sometimes say to me, "You're a wealthy guy, what the hell are you interested in all these problems for?" Well, I haven't forgotten my roots. The people for whom we advocate through the JCN are small business owners. A big part of the customer base at Home Depot is contractors and guys running small construction firms. Their hard work is what helped Home Depot succeed, but they do not have a lot of support. Small businesses do not have lobbyists to advocate on their behalf—so this is a critical part of the network's activities. During the COVID-19 pandemic, Alfredo Ortiz and Elaine Parker worked to ensure that relief funds could be distributed through banks rather than small business associations. That is just one way we have tried to give them a voice.

The blood bank, Grady Hospital, charter schools, Camp Twin Lakes, and the Job Creators Network are just a few of the hundreds of organizations we support, but each tells a story about what we believe is important. You are probably starting to see a common theme—success depends on having partners who share our do-it-yourself attitude. Our best outcomes have come from finding the right people—Jay, Pete, Tom, Pitbull, Doug, Steve, Alfredo, and Elaine—and organizations that care deeply about making things better. Good partners help leverage our impact, which in turn promotes sustainability. That is both good work and good business.

MISSIONARY ZEAL

In each of our giving areas, I have used lessons that I learned in my career—building on the concept of entrepreneurial philanthropy. You have to have a missionary's zeal for your work. Let me show you what I mean. Imagine you have a meeting at your foundation with somebody who is deeply committed about the cause they are pitching. The need is substantial. They have done their research. It fits your mission, and they have a great story. Their presentation is impressive, and they have the right people in the room making the ask. The hour is up, and as the conversation winds down they request five minutes to talk privately. When everybody else is gone, they turn to you and ask, "Are there any job openings here? I'd love to work for the foundation."

Are you kidding me? What was the whole last hour about? This has happened to me dozens of times. You cannot sell something you don't care about—and you sure as hell should not undermine a perfectly good pitch in the last few minutes. I often cannot even remember what the ask was for, but I definitely remember what they did wrong. It would be like somebody saying, "Curing pediatric leukemia is my life's work, and I'm asking for your support. By the way, are you hiring?" That is not zeal.

You also have to do your homework—in business and in giving. In 2003, I received a letter from a school in Greensboro, North Carolina, asking for $10 million for a major capital campaign. It was a huge ask from an institution that we knew nothing about. The school made no effort to set up a meeting to tell us their story or to even research whether the Marcus Foundation gave grants in this area. It probably took them less than thirty minutes to slap their ask on letterhead and throw it in the mailbox. We guessed that they probably sent the same letter to other foundations to see if they got any bites. That made it pretty easy to say no, which we did politely in a letter that took us less than five minutes to create and drop in the mail. A week later, we got a second letter from the same school, this time asking for $10,000 for a basketball hoop. What was wrong with these people?

You also have to make a compelling case for why your idea fills a real need. The headmaster at the Greensboro school could learn a few things from Ilan Regenbaum, a thirteen-year-old student from Atlanta. He called out of the blue to request a meeting with the foundation. He explained that each Jewish day school in the city sends their students to Israel in the year of their bar or bat mitzvah, and his friend could not afford the trip. Ilan had some kind of chutzpah. His mom drove him to our offices and sat in the car while he came in and made a great pitch. It was well-researched, squarely fit our mission, focused on helping others, and was passionate. When he left, we agreed to give $50,000 in scholarships to each Jewish day school in metro Atlanta, and we have been doing that for over a decade. What did Ilan have that the headmaster at the North Carolina school did not? He showed his commitment, filled a need, did his homework, and practiced and delivered a great ask. His initial request—made over a decade ago—still has a big impact. Recently, the Marcus Foundation gave a $20 million gift to support RootOne, as a further extension of Ilan's original request.

THE PROBLEM OF GREED

I don't understand some wealthy people. It is almost as though they are keeping a scorecard: Who can get richer? Who can buy a bigger plane or a fancier superyacht? Who can buy a private island? It's a perverse game of one-upsmanship. Who has time for that? I had a friend who, I discovered, was making more than $5 million, and yet gave away only $750 a year. That was it. The rest he spent on himself and boasted about it. I ended that friendship, and I'm sure he still gives nothing away and feels good about it.

Research on giving shows that some of the wealthiest Americans give about 1.3 percent of their income, but the poorest donate closer to 3.2 percent. I have to admit I am surprised, but also inspired by the fact that average, everyday people find ways to support their communities. It may be to their church. It might be to a library. It could be to a food bank. But they understand that it is essential to building a better society. Starting a small business is helpful. Supporting your family is important. Making money is nothing to be ashamed of. But so is the value of individual giving—that is what my mother did collecting coins when I was a child. But you can't just give. You can't sit back and be passive. You have to find a way to get involved and contribute your skills. If you aren't helping or volunteering, you are missing the best part of your life. That is what builds a spirit of connectedness. Nothing compares to the feeling that you get when you know you've touched somebody. Just writing a check will never give you that.

As long as I still have a heartbeat, I will continue to focus on philanthropy, but I refuse to leave my business sense at the door. I want to live to be one hundred because I want to be in a position to give to those things that I really believe in, just like my mother did more than a century ago. Her generosity, no matter how small, made a real difference in the lives of the people she touched. Inspired by her example, I use my skills as an entrepreneur to think about philanthropy as something that requires creativity, disruption, and innovative thinking. Only then can you dream big and have a real impact.

CHAPTER 9

FAILURE IS NOT FATAL

I have experienced plenty of failure in my life, from not being able to pay a bribe to Harvard Medical School to getting fired from Handy Dan. At Home Depot, we made plenty of mistakes, from buying a chain of stores in Texas that nearly bankrupted us to selling bad nails. In our giving, we struggled to build awareness for autism, refused to partner with 23andMe while developing JScreen, and experienced plenty of setbacks in medical research. But in each case, we got up, dusted ourselves off, and tried again. The best part about being in your nineties is that you don't have to soft-pedal anything. Mistakes are mistakes, failures are failures. I wrote this book because I wanted to tell you the unvarnished truth, believing that the lessons embedded in these stories can help you build your business and shape your legacy.

I've had plenty of war rooms in my career. The first was a booth in a California diner where Arthur Blank and I hashed out the concept for Home Depot. In the second, for the Georgia Aquarium, the trash cans were overflowing with ideas that we rejected. My third war room is the conference room at the Marcus Foundation where our staff and board members review thousands of proposals each year to decide how to do our best work. Each war room was different, but they all became spaces where no idea was too outlandish to consider. Try this. Didn't work. Try that. Ideas, heated debates, suggestions, flops, and detours. Over and over again, because you never know where the next big idea is going to emerge. Each war room became a place to experiment, fail, innovate, discover, and do. We don't just want to sit around and talk about things—and you shouldn't either. We should get out there and do something. In 2019, Home Depot announced a new tagline: "How Doers Get More Done." You know, I just might get that tattooed on my ass.

A TEXAS-SIZE SCREW UP

Good companies make mistakes. Big companies make mistakes. Young companies make the most mistakes. Home Depot made a whopper in 1984 that nearly destroyed us.

We had recently expanded out of the Atlanta market into South Florida and Phoenix, Arizona, and our profitability was through the roof. Looking for ways to continue to expand, we purchased real estate in California and Texas, and right before Halloween that year, we bought a Texas-based chain, Bowater Home Centers, for $38.4 million. They had nine stores in Texas, Louisiana, and Alabama that copied Home Depot. When we were starting Home Depot, we tried to sell a small equity stake to them for $2 million, but they turned us down. Now the tables were turned. When we visited the stores, we were surprised by how run-down and badly managed they were. But we believed that our management could turn things around.

We asked Bowater to become Home Depot. They sold different things, had a different corporate culture, and had employees that were not trained in the ways of things orange. We tried to absorb a company that did not share our values. What looked like a golden opportunity sapped talent out of our stores and burdened the whole company. Instead of having our best managers running great stores, we sent them to bail out these newly acquired ones that did not have the same merchandise or customer service. We asked too much of both companies and nearly went bankrupt in the process.

It all came down to culture. Our managers were engaged in their stores, walking the floor, helping associates, and troubleshooting. Bowater managers never left their offices. I remember hearing a great story from Home Depot store manager Ron McCaslin about a forklift. Frustrated by the Bowater manager's refusal to come out from behind his desk, Ron got a forklift and knocked down the walls of the office. We explained until we were blue in the face about why their hands-off approach would not work. In the end, we fired most of the Bowater executives and managers. Then we worked with individual employees to teach them the Home Depot way, hoping it would make a difference. It did not.

By this point we were a publicly traded company, beholden to Wall Street. It got so bad that I had to go to New York with Ron Brill and meet with the analysts and fund managers. We ate plenty of crow that day. I explained, "I am a schmuck. Instead of closing the Bowater stores, we tried to renovate them. That just confused the customers, made the former employees resentful, and taxed our people beyond their limits." Boy, did we pay the price. In the fourth quarter of 1984 our numbers were way down. But we knew there was nothing to be gained by covering up our mistake. We didn't come in with a slick presentation—just cold, hard numbers that showed what we did wrong. We knew that without Bowater, we would have had a thirty-five percent increase in quarterly earnings. We could have played with the numbers or tried to downplay what was happening. But we were transparent and made a promise that we would fix it, and we did. Ron and I never played games with Wall Street, and that honest reputation became worth its weight in gold.

This mistake taught us some hard lessons that can help you: Don't overstate your abilities or capacity. Do your due diligence before you make an investment or final decision. Ask tough questions of the management, vendors, shareholders, employees, and customers and be realistic about what your company can handle. We were still a young company, and it was not realistic to think we could send in talented managers and magically fix every store. We were reveling in our success and became overconfident, which bred arrogance and unrealistic expectations. Beware of your success, but also know that you have to take the long view. What looked like a failure for a few years ultimately turned around. By 1986, we started making money and became dominant in the markets where we bought the Bowater stores, especially Dallas–Fort Worth. This debacle also prompted a major change to our company's operations, and we put safeguards in place that would keep us from another risky decision that could just about kill us.

WE DON'T SELL ANY NAILS

What do most people buy in hardware stores? Light bulbs, paint, and nails. Store walks have always been the best way for me to see what was really happening at Home Depot. One day, I was in a California store, talking to customers and associates. Associates that didn't know me might think they should always act like everything is okay. Who wants to give the boss bad news? But those who had been with us for a while knew to speak up. On this particular day, I was getting a lot of "everything's fine," so I went into the parking lot and saw a customer with a big load of lumber. I stopped to help him and asked, "Hey, I see you're buying a lot of lumber. But you don't have any nails."

He replied, "Oh, I don't buy them here."

"Why?" I wondered.

"Well, they're no good. They're cheap; they bend all the time. So I go down to the local hardware store and get them there."

I walked back into the store, to the nail aisle, and it looked pristine. Not a box was missing. We had millions of nails piled to the ceiling. *Not* a good sign. I wanted our aisles to look well shopped, with stuff moved around and plenty of holes for merchandise that had been sold. What was going on? I found somebody who worked in hardware and asked, "Do you guys sell nails here?"

If he recognized me, he didn't let on. He explained, "We have them, but I won't sell them to you. They're no good. They bend. It's a real problem, so I'm really sorry. I wouldn't buy them from us, but I'll tell you where to go."

I replied, "Are you shitting me? This is Home Depot. You have to sell nails."

"Not these nails. Come with me." He grabbed a few boxes and a hammer and walked over to lumber and grabbed two boards. He handed me a nail and the hammer, and I started pounding away. He was right. They bent.

While hammering, he explained, "You know, my manager and I have been on the phone for months to the district managers and the buyers to try to get this fixed. I've even made calls to the Home Depot headquarters, and we can't seem to get it changed. So we've told the other stores in California about the problem, and they do the same thing we do—tell customers to shop elsewhere."

I couldn't believe it. What was this, *Miracle on 34th Street*, where the Macy's Santa tells customers to go to Gimbels? We were the largest home improvement company in the nation and couldn't get the right nails. We found the manager, and I said, "Pull all the nails off the shelf. I'm going to fix this." And we did. We found another manufacturer and, almost overnight, we were back in the nail business. I give the associates and manager a lot of credit for steering customers away from a defective product and trying to fix the problem on their own. But it told me that our bureaucracy was a problem—how many calls did they have to make before somebody noticed? I called Pat Farrah and he jumped on it immediately, and the nail buyer's job security ended. This incident resulted in a new policy. All our manufacturers had to send somebody to our stores for one weekend each month to talk with associates and customers about their products. That way, if there were problems, we could solve them before they rose to the level of a crisis.

The story also reminded us of our early days. In the first two or three years, we used to roam the parking lots, and if somebody walked out without a bag, we would go up to them and say, "I'm doing a survey for Home Depot. I see you didn't buy anything. What did you come in for today?" They would tell us, and we'd get their name, number, and address and tell them that we would see if we could get it. Today, that might seem odd—but I guess our orange aprons made us look trustworthy. Then we'd go to our competitor, buy it, and have it delivered but charge them twenty-five percent less than our competitor did. We kept careful records of those transactions and reviewed them at daily meetings to see what patterns emerged. It worked. We made lifelong customers and figured out right away where our blind spots were.

STRATEGIC IMPATIENCE

Sam Walton used to tell me a story about one of his biggest mistakes. When Walmart was expanding, he would take managers from one store to open the next one. At first, it seemed like a good idea—take someone with experience and have them share it with a new crew. What he learned was that these roving managers were just making the same mistakes over and over again and replicating them at all the new stores. The mistakes cost a ton of money and made the company less efficient. So he decided to train a small group that had one job—go and open new stores. They would travel around the country and replicate the Walmart way.

After a year, Sam decided to visit the group to see how things were going. But he could not find them. It turns out that the team leader had hired more than 1,000 associates and relocated them to a new building. That was not what Sam intended. He was not trying to create a massive bureaucracy with all this overhead. He wanted a nimble group that knew how to open stores, not a massive group of paper pushers. So he put an end to it and loved to end the story with his favorite punch line: Bureaucracies are like cockroaches—you can't see them until you turn on the light.

One rule of the Marcus Foundation is that we won't get involved with the government at the city, state, or federal level if we can avoid it. Like Sam, we hated red tape. It slows things down and stifles creativity—and things never get finished. We love working with entrepreneurs because they are not afraid to think big. We try to partner with people who are strategically impatient, who don't wait for someone else to try something new.

You can't expect that everything you try is going to work—new businesses, new ideas, and new treatments often fail. You might have a good business plan, but you lack the experience, resources, or knowledge to properly execute it. You might not care very much about the project or have the wrong people on your team. Your partners might have different expectations. You might have underestimated your costs. You might not have a compelling story about why your product or idea will work. But ideas that fail are not wasted. They give you valuable information that influences what you do next, and the sweetest successes come from hard work. I love the story of Thomas Edison, who struggled for three years testing different materials on his way to inventing a successful prototype for the light bulb.

When a reporter asked, "How did it feel to fail 1,000 times?"

He replied, "I didn't fail 1,000 times. The light bulb was an invention with 1,000 steps."

I would rather hire somebody who tried ten things and failed at seven than someone who only attempted two. Getting three out of ten right is not failure—it shows grit, determination, resilience, and perseverance. My work is not driven by perfection, but by experimentation. The only way to find the best solution is to try multiple approaches. When they fail, look back and figure out what went wrong, formulate a new plan, and then take a different kind of risk. Mistakes are the dues you pay on the way to success.

PUZZLE PIECES

That was certainly the case with our work on autism. It all began with a four-year-old boy. He screamed all the time, was unable to communicate, and could not do basic tasks like eating or going to the bathroom. His mother worked for me, and she had taken him to more than half a dozen doctors. They ran all kinds of tests, and she had piles of reports, but no clear answers. She approached each new appointment with a glimmer of hope, only to come back completely destroyed. She came to me out of desperation. In the late 1980s, there were no effective treatments for autism. The condition did not even appear in the *Diagnostic and Statistical Manual of Mental Disorders* (DSM) until 1987. So children with autism were doomed to a kind of medical wilderness. If things were going to change for kids who were struggling, I needed to apply the do-it-yourself mentality I learned as an entrepreneur.

Although I knew almost nothing about autism, I did know how to build things from scratch. While traveling around the country for Home Depot, I tried to schedule meetings with doctors, researchers, psychologists, and teachers. I began to grasp just how big this problem was, just how many children were being left behind. I wanted to find out what kinds of issues were stalling research and what treatment could help these kids. To that end, we started the Marcus Developmental Resource Center (now the Marcus Autism Center) in 1991. The early days were challenging, and we experienced a lot of failure, mostly because people knew so little about the condition. We determined that it was important to be affiliated with a major research university, so we ultimately entered into an agreement with Emory and started with two trailers off Chantilly Drive near their Atlanta campus. By the fourth week, we were inundated with hundreds of people and our troubles continued to grow.

The Marcus Foundation paid all the bills in the first years that the center was open, costing about $7 million a year. Each year my board would say, "Bernie, this is not sustainable. You have to close it down." So I would go to the center to meet with the staff and invariably a woman would come running over to me and hug me and say that I had saved her life. She would tell me her whole story— often eerily similar to the ones I had heard before. They had struggled going to doctors for years without any success and had lost hope. Caring for her child had taken every penny the family had, but the center had changed everything. I would go back to the foundation board and say, "No, we are keeping it open for another year." But it was clear that the center was going down the drain financially. We knew we were doing good work, but we just had to find a better model.

In 1998, the Marcus Foundation agreed to donate $45 million to the Kennedy Krieger Institute in Baltimore to help build a national network of centers around the nation, but it was not the long-term solution we had hoped for. I could write a whole book about our work with autism, but the most important thing I learned was that because the condition was not well understood, it was almost impossible to attract financial support. We had to do something to change that. In 2005, I reached out to Bob Wright, who was the president and CEO of NBC

Universal, and his wife, Suzanne. Their grandson had autism and had been treated at our center in Atlanta. They knew our work, and I thought they would be perfect for this job. I called him to ask for a meeting, and he invited me to his Rockefeller Center office. I told him, "Bob, I'd like to talk to you, but I really want your wife to join us." I knew that as the grandmother, she would have a special perspective. We finally agreed that I'd come to his house the morning that they were leaving for the Winter Olympics. I jumped into sales mode and focused all my energy on Suzanne. I knew she was brilliant and driven and that her grandson's situation was breaking her heart. I finally said, "Do you want to help start an advocacy organization? If so, I promise to give $5 million a year for five years to set it up." We were running out of time, so I jumped on the helicopter to ride with them to the airport. I was laying on all my Southern charm, and pretty soon had her in tears.

I did not know it had worked until Suzanne called me the next day. That is how Autism Speaks, the largest advocacy organization in the world for this condition, was launched. In the past two decades, they have completely changed the conversation and research landscape around autism. By building awareness around the world, they have raised over a billion dollars in funding and worked diligently to get support from insurance companies.

We eventually partnered with Children's Healthcare of Atlanta and, in 2010, hired Dr. Ami Klin, a world-renowned scientist in the autism community known for developing cutting-edge eye-tracking technology to diagnose autism in younger children. I sat on the board for five years until they were fully operational. We accomplished part of our vision, and I would say that three out of ten things that we tried worked. There were many failures, dead ends, and false starts, especially in the early years, but we now believe we provide the best clinical care for children and families anywhere in the world.

WHAT DO YOU NEED THE MONEY FOR?

Our missteps with autism resulted from being in unchartered territory; our mistake with JScreen was all about hubris. While developing this new genetic test for people of Jewish ancestry, we lost out on a big opportunity. Bringing the product to market had plenty of twists and turns, but the biggest challenge, just like with autism, was getting the word out. We took a regional approach at first, trying to make inroads into a range of organizations to help create a team of ambassadors. We toured and spoke at temples and Jewish organizations and met with community leaders. Then we started to take a national approach—hosting events in cities all over the country. We looked for key influencers in each of those cities who could help market JScreen. Even though we brought the price down to make it affordable, it was a challenge because a lot of young people think they are invincible. They are not worried about the future. It was also hard to figure out when to be tested—before you start dating, while dating, when a relationship gets serious, or do you wait until you are engaged or planning to start a family? There were so many issues, and I think we could have done a much better job promoting it in the early years.

One day, out of the blue, Jay got a call from Anne Wojcicki, the founder of 23andMe and then-wife of Google co-founder Sergey Brin. She asked for a meeting, so we selected a date, and Jay and I flew to California. Anne had a big pitch: She wanted us to merge with her company. She had a national network and an infrastructure that would have made it possible to scale JScreen. She had a great advertising campaign, and we could have done ten times the amount of testing that we were doing. It would have taken us out of the picture, but what difference did that make if the work was being done? We did not need the credit, we just wanted people to get screened in a safe, affordable, and confidential way. But there was one problem. JScreen was a nonprofit and 23andMe was a for-profit company. That was a dealbreaker. We kept asking her, "What do you need the money for?" But it was my mistake. I got so hung up on the idea of it being a nonprofit that I lost sight of the importance of building a company that could really reach a wide audience. JScreen is not a failure, but it could have served more young people and been much bigger had I not been so stubborn. In this case, we saw a problem and solved it but not as successfully as we could have. We would have been better together, but we haven't given up. JScreen is now head-quartered at Emory University's Department of Human Genetics, and it currently tests for sixty-three genetic defects and forty types of cancers. I like to think of it as a work in progress.

FAILURE IS BAKED IN

As you can see, the Marcus Foundation's medical philan-thropy portfolio is different from our other four funding areas. Medical research is complicated, costly, and time consuming, and failure is baked in. We have had plenty of firsthand experience with this, and we bring to it the same do-it-yourself attitude that we used at Home Depot. Success is rare, and a lot of people ask me why I bother with this kind of research. Why take such big risks at this point in my life? I think it's just part of my DNA. From my pharmacy training, I know that a lot of things work, even if they haven't been formally tested. If we can save one life, we've made a difference. This is tough work that requires a thick skin, but it's worth the gamble because among the dozens of failures are some real breakthroughs. Let me show you what I mean.

There is a concept in medicine—bench to bedside—that describes the conventional process by which the results of research done in a laboratory help develop new ways to treat patients. In our philanthropy, we look for organizations, doctors, and hospitals that are willing to turn that concept on its head. Plasma therapy seemed to offer some promise for COVID-19 patients. There seemed to be a benefit, now we had to find out why. That bedside observation led to a clinical study. Looking closely at something that was working in the field, then developing a research protocol to understand why, has brought about some of the most innovative and cutting-edge solutions in medicine, or what we call bedside to bench.

We have become deeply invested in areas that embrace this approach, and one of the most exciting is integrative health. This concept draws upon conventional, complementary, and alternative medicines and treatments. I found out about it from a Canadian friend who lived in Atlanta. She had been facing an invasive surgery and wanted a second opinion. She reached out to Dr. George

Zabrecky, who had a reputation for trying unconventional but highly effective treatments. She went to meet with him; he took her off all her medications and started a homeopathic therapy that helped her recover.

I heard this story from my friend just when I needed it. My daughter was in Boston making a living as a musician and became very ill. Nobody could figure out what was wrong, even after visiting half a dozen doctors. Some suggested she was imagining it all and needed a psychiatrist. One day, while riding her bicycle, she started to develop second-degree burns on her skin. Terrified by this unusual symptom, I called George, and he agreed to drive to Boston to see her. After several tests, he determined that she had severe lead poisoning. His quick diagnosis and treatment saved her life. Then, it was my turn.

I was in Florida playing golf with Billi and stopped at a cooler between holes to get some cold water. I quickly came down with a violent case of diarrhea. It was so bad that I lost fourteen pounds in four days. I was dehydrated and felt like I was going to die. I had an excellent team of doctors, and they all had different suggestions—try this, try that, triple your dosage of this medication, switch to that medication. It nearly killed me. So I called George, and he came to see me. He diagnosed me with giardia, a microscopic parasite that can come from contaminated food or water. He suggested that I take two pills that had been made from a root native to the Amazon a day for three days. I did, and I was soon back to normal. What was extraordinary about George was that he was willing to look at all options and was not attempting to solve every problem with a new prescription. He also tries, like we do, to find effective solutions that are affordable for everybody. Who cares that you have a great treatment if it is so expensive that only the wealthiest people can try it? George also helped me treat a lung condition using stem cells, and for years I traveled to Panama for treatments that had not yet been approved by the FDA. Now, stem cells are widely used, and the Marcus Foundation supports research and clinical trials to help with everything from autism to COVID-19.

George inspired us to fund a promising study that examined whether vitamin C, thiamine, and steroids could improve outcomes for patients in septic shock, a dangerous and often fatal condition. The hope was that the antioxidant and anti-inflammatory properties of the cocktail could save their life. This was for patients who had days to live, and we developed a study involving researchers and patients at multiple universities. The article published in the *Journal of the American Medical Association* (*JAMA*) in 2019 revealed a study flaw. Instead of focusing on patients on the verge of death, it studied the effect of the cocktail on sepsis more generally. While the generalized data was inconclusive, the outcome for seriously ill patients held promise. Simply put: We designed a bad study. Now we have to go back to the drawing board and be clearer about the outcome we are looking for. In the process, we also learned that a good idea does not always result in new treatments. There was no money to be made because the drugs in the cocktail were widely available and cost less than $23—so investors and pharmaceutical companies didn't show any interest. This is a big conundrum—here was an affordable, easy to manufacture combination of drugs and vitamins that could save lives. But drug testing and distribution is expensive, and if it can't be patented, there is no profit to be made. As a result, people suffer. But we didn't give up. In honor of my good friend Shalom Neuman, we funded an entire floor in a clinic in New York for vitamin C infusions. Every day, it improves the quality of life for cancer patients who desperately need help.

I can't count how many times my friends and colleagues have rolled their eyes at me when I talk about our medical philanthropy. One of my doctors tells me that our work on stem cells is not science but voodoo, as if we were swinging around chicken bones. I understand the heavy reliance on data, well-constructed studies, and trials, but I don't understand the refusal to even consider an entrepreneurial approach. If a cocktail of commonly available vitamins and generic drugs will solve a problem, why not try it? Many of these same people who were once skeptical call me in moments of desperation—their wife, daughter, son, or friend is dying and has tried every conventional treatment. Is there anything else we can recommend? They are begging for referrals to universities and physicians who are doing integrative research. They were hesitant until they were faced with losing somebody they loved. They often find success with integrative medicine and call to thank me later. I love hearing these stories because you never know where the next big idea will come from, and if three of them end up saving thousands or even millions of lives, shouldn't we take a chance?

Despite such frustrations, there is a light at the end of the tunnel. We have expanded our focus to include late-stage cancers where the outcomes are particularly grim. There are some promising new therapies for neuroblastoma that mainly affects children. We are also funding research on developing T-cell adoptive therapies for lymphoma at the City of Hope in Los Angeles, stem cells that kill infected or cancer cells at M.D. Anderson in Houston, and an early detection blood test at the Johns Hopkins Kimmel Cancer Center in Baltimore. The liquid biopsy test at Hopkins could be a game changer—it can detect twenty-six different cancers in the early, asymptomatic stages. Think about it: More than two-thirds of cancers could be detected during your routine physical before any symptoms appear. Detecting cancer in stage 1 instead of stage 4 can be the difference between life and death. This will substantially reduce suffering and death for millions of people. I've lost some of my dearest friends to this disease, so if there is something that could have saved their lives earlier, don't you think it's worth it? The test is currently under review by the FDA, and we are hopeful it will be made available soon.

FAIL BETTER

One thing that saved us in business and giving was that we were never really impressed with ourselves. We always look for flaws, weaknesses, and ways to improve. I knew that complacency, like kudzu, can strangle an organization's culture, and by the time you realize it, you're buried under the vines. At Home Depot, we visited our competitors, talked to our customers, listened to complaints, tried new merchandising techniques, and tested new technologies. At the Marcus Foundation, we ask tough questions, leverage our giving to encourage others to join, try to expand and deepen partnerships, and take big risks. Some things work, but many do not. We did and still do postmortem meetings at Home Depot and the

Marcus Foundation to discuss what happened, what we could have changed, and what we learned from our failure. Then, using that experience and knowledge, we take the next big risk. This has helped create an entrepreneurial culture where we acknowledge fumbles with the goal of doing better.

I have learned that failure sometimes results in a much-needed detour because circumstances change, new opportunities arise, or the original approach just doesn't work. The key is to not let your ego overwhelm your common sense—admit what's not working and try something else. Bouncing back and being willing to pivot can get you across the finish line. I do not dwell on the past with regret, nor do I spend a lot of time worrying about blame. Instead, I want to try the next big thing with the hope that it might provide new knowledge and discovery. We failed sometimes because we made a bad decision— like Bowater. Other times, it was because we didn't have the right team. But more often we failed because we experimented with something and bumped up against problems or opportunities we had not foreseen. You only do that when you take big chances. Samuel Beckett once said, "Try again. Fail again. Fail better." That's just the kind of advice I can get behind.

Being open to new ideas, embracing the need to constantly pivot, and understanding that you are lucky if three out of ten things work has been an important key to our success. This is the very opposite of bureaucracy—which results in mounds of paper and lost opportunities, and not much else. I have always refused to do things because "that's the way it has always been done." People ask me all the time: Why are you planning to dissolve the Marcus Foundation twenty years after you die? Why quit? I don't see it as a failure to sunset our giving. We give wisely and try to do good work right now. We give the moment we see a need. Maybe another way to ask the question is: What counts as success? I would argue that it's when you don't wait for others to do the hard work. Get out there and do it yourself.

CHAPTER 10

WE ARE IN THE SELLING BUSINESS

All good companies tell a good story—why their product or service will make your life better. Walmart saves you money. Zoom connects you to colleagues from the comfort of your home or office. CVS is a one-stop shop for healthcare. Nonprofits, too: The Salvation Army fights for the good, and M.D. Anderson is making cancer history. I've seen many businesses and great causes fail because the founders can't articulate why their idea or product is worth buying. This is a failure of storytelling.

You don't want to be the pharmaceutical rep who couldn't explain why this new drug can make a difference and loses a $4 million account. You don't want to be the entrepreneur who can't articulate the value of their start-up to a room full of venture capitalists. You don't want to be the head of a nonprofit who is unable to explain why their work matters and see a major gift go to a competitor. We are in the selling business, and all businesses and causes need a great story. Learn it. Practice it. Master it. Let me show you how.

A good story needs a good hook. Every good hook needs three things: passion, an emotional connection, and the ability to communicate purpose and value in simple terms. What grabs your attention and makes people want to invest their time and energy? I hear all the time, "I am a terrible salesperson," or "I hate to ask for money." This anxiety masks some important truths. Everybody cares about something, and they want to convince others to support them. Great salespeople know that stories, not facts or statistics, have the most powerful impact on someone's emotions and ultimately motivate them to act. The customer may not remember every detail, but they will remember how a story made them feel.

I WAS GREAT AT THIS

Years ago, when I worked for Daylin, the co-founder Amnon Barness called me into his office. As I approached the door, I heard him yelling in what sounded like

Hebrew. He motioned for me to come into the room and sit down. I could not understand what was being said, but it sounded like a terrific argument. When he finished, I asked if everything was okay. He looked at me oddly and explained, "That was Golda Meir."

Curiosity got the better of me, and I had to ask, "What were you arguing about?"

"Oh, we weren't arguing," he laughed. "That's how Israelis talk."

I still wasn't sure why he had asked me in. Finally, he explained.

"Every year, we raise funds for Israel Bonds—an idea pioneered by the country's first prime minister, David Ben-Gurion, after the 1948 War of Independence. I'm going to give you some good leads to see if you can drum up some support." I agreed to try, but had no idea what I was doing. I had never asked for money before, had no experience in development, and was terrified.

After a bunch of cold calls that led nowhere, an executive from one of the big manufacturing companies in New York City invited me to a board meeting to make my pitch. I think he sensed my desperation and felt a little sorry for me. While I was waiting to speak, I looked around the conference room table and started to wonder: Why would these guys care about supporting a country halfway around the world that they know nothing about?

But I have a big mouth, and when it was my turn, I started talking about how their support would help the single democracy in the Middle East that the United States needed. I knew from my time working as a comedian and hypnotist in the Catskills that I wasn't exactly killing it.

Ten minutes into my spiel, I finally turned to the chairman and asked, "Are there any Jews in this room?" Everybody looked a little embarrassed, but nobody raised their hand. This was a really big company, so it was hard to believe they had no Jewish employees. But I kept going. "Israel is one of our biggest allies, and we need to help them. They are our best friend in the region, and this is the right thing to do." I went on and on and closed by asking for their support. I do not recall the exact amount of my ask, but I think it was a million dollars. They led me out of the room, and I sat in the lobby dejected, trying to think about what on earth I could have done better. Finally, they brought me back and said they would buy two million in bonds—twice what I had requested. I couldn't believe it! What had I been so worried about? I was great at this! That thought lasted for about ten seconds. Something didn't seem right, and I was puzzled. Could it really be that easy?

I thanked the board and made some small talk, but felt like I had to ask the blunt question, "Why did you buy so much?" The chairman explained that I had made a good case, and they were all a little embarrassed that they hadn't even thought about the issue.

The lessons I learned that day? Don't be discouraged if you fail and don't take all the credit when you succeed. I had no experience at fundraising, but found myself at the right place at the right time and made my case in simple terms. The real lesson is that the only way to get lucky is to grind away and remember the immortal words of Winston Churchill, "Success is not final, failure is not fatal, it is the courage to continue that counts." I still laugh about that moment—all these years later, it has kept me humble. It also taught me how to get to the heart of an issue. That is what makes a great story.

HELL, I WAS CRYING

Sometimes a good story does not resonate right away. When I was the CEO of Handy Dan, I attended a fundraiser for the City of Hope. This facility near Los Angeles was founded in 1913 and offers free medical care for patients struggling with life-threatening diseases. That night, they were honoring executives from our parent company, Daylin Corporation, for our giving. It was about the fifth evening event I had on my calendar that week, and I was not looking forward to another rubber chicken dinner. Much of the evening was not terribly memorable, but when the City of Hope CEO came to the podium he started telling amazing stories of how their work had turned around even the most hopeless cases. His final words stuck with me: "We solve problems that others cannot. We have dozens of clinical trials that have saved people's lives who have been given no hope. Your donations fund hope." Powerful ask, I thought. They identified a need, told an inspirational story, and made a strategic request for support. Little did I know that I was about to learn, in a very personal way, that they also delivered.

Fast forward a few months. One day, one of my regional managers came to see me. He told me he had to resign. He was a great employee, and when I asked him why, he started crying hysterically. When he finally caught his breath, he told me that he had a rare form of cancer, was given six weeks to live by his doctor, and was there to quit his job so he could put his affairs in order. He was barely thirty, had a wife and young child, and was out of his mind with grief and anxiety. We sat there for a while—now we were both crying—not sure what do to. Then it hit me—the fundraising dinner. The CEO. My manager. The hope. I picked up the phone to call City of Hope to ask for help, and without hesitation, the CEO said, "Send him right over." The story of how they saved his life is amazing, but what happened next made all the difference.

I was so impressed by their entire operation that I asked if I could join their board. I had never been on a board before or done much with philanthropy. I did not have much money, but I could donate my time. In 1982, a small group of executives formed the Hardware/Home-building Industry (HHI), and City of Hope was one of our beneficiaries. By this time, Home Depot was four years old. The HHI held their annual fundraiser on Tuesday night at the annual International Builders Show, and all the big stores were there—Lowe's, Sears, and Home Depot. One year, I chaired the event, and we were in the ballroom of the Chicago Hilton. A staff member from the City of Hope told a heartbreaking story of a woman dying from an aggressive form of cancer. She was in a wheelchair, had stopped eating, and could barely function. She came to the City of Hope, underwent a bone marrow transplant, and the next slide showed a picture of her smiling with her children. The next thing we knew, the spotlight left the podium, swept over the crowd to the back of the room, and this woman jumped up and started running toward the stage. I was the chairman of the event, and this was a total surprise, even to me. The impact on the audience was unbelievable. People were crying. Hell,

I was crying. Her life had been saved, and she was right here to tell us about it. I was hooked, and I trace my philosophy of giving to that single moment.

That night showed that the City of Hope had passion, filled a need, and was changing medicine. But nobody would have cared if they had not made a compelling case about why their work mattered. The cancer survivor running to the podium was a great hook—and everybody in that audience made a donation that night. You know how I know it was good? I am still talking about it today.

GOING FOR THE GOLD

At Home Depot, we gave to causes in our community that supported our values. That's why in 1996 we became a sponsor for the Summer Olympics in Atlanta. Almost everybody expected the Games to be awarded to Greece because it was the centennial of the modern Olympics, but the International Olympic Committee (IOC) selected Atlanta. The chairman of the Atlanta committee, Billy Payne, persuaded us to be a lead sponsor at $40 million. That was a huge commitment for us, and we could have done a lot with that money—like open three new stores. But Arthur and I have always been patriotic, and we felt that Atlanta had helped us build Home Depot, so we should give back to the city in a big way as they prepared to welcome the world. The best part of the experience was hiring Olympians and helping them reach their dreams through the Olympic Job Opportunity Program. We felt that Home Depot was uniquely poised to help. We had a lot of stores around the nation and offered flexible schedules. We believed that no Olympic athlete should have to choose between training and work, so we hired them and subsidized their salaries. They worked an average of twenty hours per week and were paid for forty. The rest of the time they used for training. We didn't feel like it was charity, but rather an investment in people who brought a unique work ethic to our company. Associates and customers alike loved their stories.

The Olympic values aligned nicely with ours, and leading up to the 1996 Games, more than a hundred Olympic hopefuls became Home Depot associates. Twenty-eight of them made the team and six of them medaled. We ended up hosting more job program athletes than any other company and expanded it to include the Canadian and U.S. Paralympic teams. Arthur loved to say, "The challenge to be the very best is the heart and spirit of the Olympics, and it's the heart and spirit of our company." In total, Home Depot sponsored the program for sixteen years and hired more than six hundred athletes, who brought home 145 medals. It ended in 2009 long after I retired, a casualty of the recession, but we felt that the Olympic spirit reflected our values. It was an easy sell.

Our sponsorship also told the world another story—that Home Depot had arrived. Coca-Cola had sponsored the Olympics since 1928, making it the longest-standing partner of the games. They were truly a global company; we were not yet there. We did not have stores throughout the U.S. until the 1990s, so before the 1996 Games, we could not have afforded to sign on as a sponsor. We knew from market research that Olympic sponsors are like Olympic athletes—perceived to be the top of their field. Our sponsorship signaled that we were now one of the big dogs. And it didn't hurt that the Olympic Games remain some of the most watched television programs globally. The sponsorship and everything that went with it told a powerful story about Home Depot—we were in it to win it.

HOW TO TELL A GREAT STORY

Ever since I started working retail at Two Guys, I discovered that I loved selling and could never work for a company I did not believe in—at least not for long. I also learned the hard way that you have to be honest with the customer about what the company can truly provide, even if you lose a sale. Figure out how to explain in simple terms why you deserve their business. At Home Depot, we told a powerful story without even opening our mouths. Walk into any store and you saw value in every aisle. Friendly associates were there to help, and you were going to save money. Same story, over and over again.

But not everybody is a great storyteller, and many businesses and nonprofits do it badly. The ability to articulate why your product or cause matters in a meaningful and memorable fashion can be the difference between success and failure. This is not just about sales and marketing. It is about values. What honest stories best represent who you are? Do your associates and customers tell stories that align with yours? There are practical strategies for crafting a story—to help you understand your audience and keep it simple—that will inspire and motivate.

Dig deep. Most of the storytelling that businesses and nonprofits do is inauthentic; it feels like something that was crafted in a boardroom. The hard work of building a business or helping a community solve a problem rarely fits into neat and tidy packages. This is not some after-school special. You have to craft a story that ties your value proposition to an emotional connection. That is why the City of Hope story early in my career worked. They made a promise to treat incurable diseases, and their long battles are the big story. The cancer patient that had no chance of survival running to the podium was a powerful illustration of why their work mattered.

Be memorable. Most people don't remember slogans or taglines unless they are great—like Just Do It or America Runs on Dunkin'. Big organizations have a challenge—they are faceless and largely generic. People aren't usually moved by statistics, facts, or figures. They don't care about your balance sheet or annual report. They are looking for connections to their own lives—how can you help them make it better? They respond to human stories that pack a punch. The old adage—people don't remember what you say, they remember how you made them feel—rings true in business and in philanthropy.

Warts and all. The best stories are the ones that don't shy away from difficult issues. Success is rarely as interesting as the struggle. I am no diplomat, so I rarely airbrush the truth. That got me into some trouble in my career, but it makes for a great story because people can relate. I'm not Mr. Marcus, the CEO. I'm Bernie, the guy who failed as a hypnotist in the Catskills. Building a billion-dollar business is great, but I will always remember our kids giving out $1 bills at our first stores trying to drum up business. I love telling the story about getting fired at forty-nine—not because it was pleasant, but because it forced me to take the biggest risk of my life. Stories must create a personal connection. That is why Nike is so successful—almost all of their television spots have featured professional athletes you admire ("You Can't Be Stopped," 2020) or average people that look like you ("Find Your Greatness," 2012). Both work because they tell the same great story—that you can do it.

FORTY-FIVE MINUTES

It takes about forty-five minutes. You can set your watch. Every week, we receive between seventy-five and a hundred calls at the Marcus Foundation seeking funding. We meet with a small percentage of those. There is another subset of people who make an appointment ostensibly to say hello. They often are casual acquaintances and simply tell us that they "just want to drop by." Those meetings always follow the same trajectory. There is some small talk. Ask about the grandchildren. Stall. About forty-five minutes into the conversation, the person finally gets to the point. More often than not, they stumble around trying to act like they are not there to ask for money. They apologize. They hedge. They name drop. It's like a slow-motion car crash—it's painful but it's also hard to look away. Jay Kaiman and I often try to stop the bleeding by asking, "Why are you here?" We are trying to get them to explain why their cause is important, why it would make somebody's life better, and why it matters. But mostly we are just trying to get them to be honest and tell their story. Don't lie about your visit. Don't act like you are just "in the neighborhood." Be bold and explain what you need and why. Success depends on making your intentions clear. Otherwise, nobody will trust you.

I had a similar experience with the president of Rutgers after we founded Home Depot. He asked me to give a business school speech, but it became really obvious that he wanted to ask me to donate millions to name a building. Here is what he should have done: Invite me to give the speech. Introduce me to his leadership team at a reception afterward. Write me a thank-you note. Get to know my story, then in a few months, reach out again and ask me to join a committee or alumni board so I could learn about the school's priorities. Ask me to do another speech for a different college or spearhead an initiative. Each step would have cultivated a relationship that was already built on loyalty to the school. I had two degrees from Rutgers and would likely have become an enthusiastic donor. I was the very definition of low-hanging fruit. Instead, he pulled a bait and switch. I have donated millions to colleges and universities all over the United States for the past thirty years—Johns Hopkins, Emory, Case Western, and Duke. Notice that Rutgers is not on the list.

Both of these stories are about integrity. I used to joke with George Shultz that I was no diplomat. I like to tell it like it is, but I also know that all great stories have to tell a universal truth. You have to find a human connection. It has to stick. Israel Bonds was all about my inexperience. City of Hope was about believing in the impossible and making it happen. Home Depot's sponsorship of the Olympics showed that we had finally arrived. The final two stories are about telling the truth. We are in the selling business, and the ability to tell a good, honest story can make or break you.

CHAPTER 11

GIVING IS BETTER THAN GETTING

I have almost died twice. The first time, Billi and I were in Atlanta on our way to dinner at an Italian restaurant on a cold wintry night in the early 1990s. We were driving on a dark, windy road, and suddenly a man in a white shirt appeared in the middle of the road waving his hands frantically to get us to stop. I slowed down, and when I got close enough, I rolled down the window to find out what was happening. The guy explained that a huge tree had fallen around the next curve, and it was blocking the road. There were live wires everywhere. Had he not been there, we would have plowed right into it. I turned to start backing up when I heard Billi yell, "Holy shit!" The next thing I knew, a car was flying through the air right toward us. The driver had hit the tree coming from the other direction. I can still see his terrified face in the windshield. He hit our hood and destroyed both of our cars. He was pretty banged up, and, luckily, we managed to walk away without any injuries. That man in the white shirt saved our lives.

The second time, in the late 1990s, was in Chicago. I was riding to O'Hare International Airport in a taxi, and a car flipped off an overpass and landed in front of us. Several people were in the car, and they were crushed by the weight. Everybody slammed on their brakes, and some truckers jumped out of their rigs with axes and fire extinguishers to help. Once the firetrucks arrived, we were able to inch our way out of the accident and proceed to the airport. My cabdriver was paralyzed with fear, so I got behind the wheel to drive. I pulled up to the departure gate, found a police officer to help get him home, and ran to my plane. Had we been traveling two seconds faster, that car would have landed on us, and we both would have been killed.

Both accidents were stark reminders that life can change in the snap of a finger. So do all you can while you're here, and don't go looking for trouble. I always wanted to learn to ski or skydive but was afraid that it would put me out of commission. I take risks for purpose, not pleasure. A lot of people depend on me, and I want to be useful because I have a lot left to give.

A LITTLE MORE MONEY

Looking at me today, it may be hard to believe that I grew up in poverty in Newark. Some nights we had only broth—no noodles, no chicken. But everybody around us was poor, so it didn't seem like a big deal. We didn't know anybody who was rich. We had an uncle who was better off than we were but we rarely saw him. Even with the little we had, our house was filled with love, and my mother taught me to be generous. She believed that the more you give, the more you get. When I asked about the few coins that went into the *pushke* box each week, she would reply, "God is good. Maybe this week, he will give us a little extra money so I can put in a little more." I didn't understand why this was so important to her, so she went on in her broken English: "You will do things I can only dream about. You could be president. Then, you, too, can help people you'll never meet." This crippled Ukrainian woman was pretty smart. She was a naturalized citizen, really believed in the American Dream, and had high hopes for all her children.

I *was* able do things that my parents could only dream about, and in my retirement have focused on helping those I will never meet, just like my mother predicted. Cancer and stroke patients, veterans, children with autism, visitors to the Georgia Aquarium—millions of them. Some people never stop trying to grow their wealth. They endlessly accumulate, reminding me of the gangster Johnny Rocco in the Humphrey Bogart 1948 film *Key Largo*. When asked by Frank McCloud what he wants, Johnny replies, "More. That's right. I want more." I see wealthy friends who have retired keep investing in new business ventures—but not spending any time or energy giving to worthy causes. I don't have time to make another fortune, and how much more could we possibly use? My family is comfortable, and now I focus all my energy on giving it all away.

A LITTLE MAKES A BIG DIFFERENCE

My approach to philanthropy, like my approach to business, has always had a do-it-yourself quality. The story of why we started the Homer Fund at Home Depot in 1999 shows that it is not hard to get people what they need right now. I received a call one day from an associate who told me he did not have enough money to pay for his parent's funeral and asked me personally for help. That affected me deeply. It is hard enough to lose a parent, but can you imagine not being able to give them a decent burial? I called a few of our managers to see if things like this were a common problem. We paid our people well, but our managers told story after story about how they occasionally struggled with unexpected expenses. As the company grew, so did our associates' needs. So I called Kenny Langone and said, "I'm going to give $5 million to start an emergency fund for our associates. Will you join me?" He agreed. Then I called Arthur with the same request. Within a few days, we had $15 million and started the Homer Fund. The fund is available to all Home Depot associates to help pay for medical bills and car repairs, cover expenses if a spouse is laid off, find shelter after a natural disaster—anything they need to help them get back on their feet. We wanted to make sure there was no shame in asking for help. So every time we talked about the fund, we made one thing crystal clear: We cared and wanted to create a safety net that told them their well-being mattered to us.

There are thousands of stories about how the fund helped people when they needed it most. I retired more than twenty years ago, and I still click on the website to watch the videos. Every few months, there is a new story: how Shelly fought brain cancer, how Jo supported her eleven-year-old nephew, how Miracle offered care for her autistic son during COVID, and how Ray, a retired medic from the Army, survived a monthlong coma and half a dozen surgeries. Arthur, Ken, and I started the Homer Fund, but we don't sustain it—that is what makes it so great. Today, the company still makes a generous donation, but so do more than ninety-five percent of the associates. The belief is that Home Depot is a family—and that if you can help your brothers and sisters when they need it most, we are all stronger. Our gift inspired their gifts, and it has inspired others. Not long after we founded the Homer Fund, Lowe's created the Lowe's Employee Relief Fund with the same basic goal. In 2012, Chef Ryan Hidiger, known for his work at well-known Atlanta restaurants Bacchanalia, Floataway Café, and Muss & Turner's, was diagnosed with late-stage cancer. The restaurant community came together to offer his family support, and his wife, Jen, believes to this day that the outpouring of love from friends and strangers alike helped extend his life by six months. Jen went on to co-found the Giving Kitchen, and they modeled it on the Homer Fund after meeting the Home Depot team. Our idea spawned others, and we hope many more. I loved it—I wish every company would do the same thing. That is exactly what entrepreneurial philanthropy can and should do.

THE HIGHEST LEVEL

Sometimes our giving is big, but sometimes it's small and personal. Maimonides, the great twelfth-century rabbi from Cairo, believed that there were eight levels of charitable giving. He prized anonymous gifts to anonymous recipients, using the example of the chamber in the ancient Temple where people would place gifts, and others could secretly come and take what they needed. But this was not the highest level of giving—that honor was reserved for someone who establishes a personal relationship with the needy person and helps in a way that does not make them feel subordinate.

At the Marcus Foundation, we've never liked blind gifts, because they prevent the donor from becoming involved in solving a problem. You can't "do it yourself" if nobody knows who you are. While all nonprofits need money, they also need expertise and advocacy. And if you give anonymously, it's difficult to bring other people on board. But we make one exception for the Salvation Army. Your house burns, you lose your job, your mother dies with unpaid bills—what do you do? Well, some people called the Marcus Foundation, and we don't do individual giving, but still wanted to help. That's when Billi suggested the Salvation Army. They have a fascinating history—founded in 1865 by Methodist minister William Booth in the East End of London as the Christian Mission. Their mission—to help those in need—has changed very little in the intervening years. I have a lot of respect for the personal nature of their work—they are on the front line of helping the people who need it the most. The Atlanta chapter does their homework and allots money. We have given millions for more than a decade to help people in our own backyard—because it is important to give where you live. I guess our gift is not so anonymous now.

SOME PEOPLE LIKE TO READ BALANCE SHEETS; I LOVE impact reports that show why our work matters. These stories stick with me. They motivate me to get up in the morning. Like Rebecca Schlegelmilch, who retired from the U.S. Army after five deployments and twenty-one years of service. She found herself completely unprepared for civilian life, and as she struggled with a traumatic brain injury (TBI), her mental health began to deteriorate. Overwhelmed by fear and anxiety, she was finding it difficult to do even the most basic everyday tasks, like showering and getting dressed. She ran into dead end after dead end trying to navigate our complicated healthcare and insurance systems. She was finally told about the Shepherd Center's SHARE Military Initiative. She started in January 2021, and she worked for twelve weeks with a team of therapists to combat the symptoms of her TBI, PTSD, anxiety, and depression. She started to feel like herself again and even learned to play the guitar. She explained that "SHARE changed my outlook by giving me hope and belief in the future. It was an amazing experience. I would highly recommend this program. If you can just get there, it can change your life. The hardest part is taking that first step." Part of the reason we started the Avalon Network was to make it possible for any veteran in the United States to have access to the same great programs free of charge. Where you live should not determine whether you survive.

I love seeing billboards around Atlanta that proclaim: "I wouldn't be here without Grady." And I know just what they mean. The Marcus Stroke and Neuroscience Center at Grady Hospital is one of the premier neuroscience centers in the world, and there are thousands of people who would not be with us but for the heroic work of doctors and nurses who know that every second counts. Just ask Tracie Steadman. On October 7, 2011, forty-three-year-old Tracie fell out of bed and couldn't get up. She said, "My whole life flashed before my eyes. I didn't know if I was going to live or die." She didn't know it at the time, but she was having a stroke. She was rushed to the Marcus Stroke and Neuroscience Center, where physicians used the latest techniques to stop her brain damage in its tracks, reversing symptoms of stroke almost immediately. She explained what happened: "Before I even got off the table, I could move my arm. I was only there for two days. I didn't need any physical therapy. I didn't even need a wheelchair. Those doctors saved my life." Mardeen Mitchell tells a similar story: "I didn't know what was happening to me. My body felt like lead. I didn't know I was having a stroke. And Dr. Nogueira went into the artery in my brain and sucked out those blood clots. How cool is that. Thank you, my Grady heroes, for making me whole again." We have given millions to Grady to make sure people like Tracie and Mardeen are still with us. Their stories and the smiling faces on the billboards are all the thanks anyone needs.

It's hard not to get hugged. When we walk into the Marcus Autism Center, a mom often sees me, runs over, and gives me a tearful, bear hug of thanks. She doesn't have to speak—I know what this is all about. We celebrate success stories every day. Like Ainsley, who was diagnosed with autism as a toddler and soon began having severe behavioral issues. She participated in the center's toilet training and feeding programs, and the language and learning clinic. Learning to communicate has altered her whole world. And Conner, who taught himself to read at the age of two. His extraordinary intelligence masked a number of developmental issues. His mom remembers that because he was an only child, they did not have enough experience. After several visits to various pediatricians and a call from a concerned preschool teacher, they brought Conner to us, and he was diagnosed with Asperger's syndrome. For the next seven years, he received daily therapy and today he is an independent teenager who does his own laundry, speaks Spanish, and is preparing for college. These children remind me that our work changes lives in a profound way.

NOT DEAD YET

It happens a lot. I'm in line at Subway getting a tuna sandwich, and the guy in front of me offers to pay for my lunch because his job at Home Depot helped put his three kids through college. We are eating at the Atlanta Fish Market, and the adjacent table picks up our tab for dinner for helping to save their child's life. Hang out with me, and you just might get a free meal. My work has made me pretty recognizable, and a lot of people enjoy saying thank you.

But what they don't know is that I'm the one who

feels an overwhelming sense of gratitude. I have been really lucky to find my passion in both business and philanthropy. That passion has kept me humming along, and in May 2019 I turned ninety and received a 111-page single-spaced document of messages from Home Depot associates. Reading them makes me feel like my life has mattered—that Home Depot mattered—that the culture we created mattered—that having a heart in business matters. I think my mother would be proud if she could see them:

Store 6204 (Norwalk, Connecticut): "Happy birthday, Bernie! Your mother said it best. You have to roll with the punches in life, success is not for the faint of heart or those who nurse grudges or harbor ill feelings toward others made in the image of God. We need to work with others to improve how we do business and listen to every worker's and customer's voice!"

David M., Store 6963 (Huntington Beach, California): "Wishing you a very happy birthday, Bernie! Thank you for creating such a wonderful company. I started with Home Depot in 1990, where I met my wife, and we have both been working for Home Depot for a combined 55 years! We started in New York and are now in California. Blessings to you on your birthday!"

Steve B., Store 1937 (Schererville, Indiana): "Thank

you for turning the loss of one job and using your vision to the future. Not only did you think of yourself and your family, but you also take care of all your associates at all the Home Depots. Thanks to your vision, when I was losing my job at Montgomery Ward as an appliance salesman, Home Depot came in and offered me my best job ever in January 2001. I have now worked with this great company for 18 years now. Bernie, I wish you a very happy birthday full of fun. I also wish you many more years."

Donald M., Store 3604 (Greensboro, North Carolina): "Happy Birthday! The Homer Fund helped me get an apartment when my wife and I were homeless with our first child on the way. This company has continued to show its gratitude for my presence and hard work. I can't thank you enough for having an entrepreneurial mindset to achieve your goals and help others succeed along the way. This company is by far the best company I have worked for."

Brad B., Store 6652 (Napa, California): "Bernie, you have changed the lives of countless people. You are a remarkable person and living 90 years—wow dude! I want to thank you for changing my life, and I truly hope you have a happy birthday with many more to come!"

We did not start Home Depot or start giving for the applause or the thanks, but I am heartened to see that something we built and supported has helped people. I couldn't hope to do better than that.

THE SCIENCE BEHIND IT

The feeling that you are helping others is priceless, and nobody can experience that feeling from a coffin. I am a pretty good businessman, and we want to work right now to try to make things better. Most charities are doing important work, but if we think we can help them be more effective, serve more people, or leverage their resources, then we get involved. Sometimes we are able to help them double or triple their outcomes. That is our job now. But we also talk to other business leaders and philanthropists and try to encourage them to become more involved. I recently had a conversation with one of the wealthiest men in America. He told me that he donates very little. When I asked why, he said, "It doesn't interest me."

I replied, "Well, what will you do with your money when you're gone?"

I was surprised to hear him say, "I guess I'll leave it to charity. I haven't thought much about it."

I kept pushing him. "You could really raise the bar for philanthropy in any area you wanted. You could help cure cancer. Look what Michael Milken did for prostate cancer. You could be five times more effective. If you decided to give, others would join you because you have so much influence. For every dollar you put in, you could probably leverage five or ten more dollars. Just think about it."

But I could not convince him, and he will never realize how valuable he could be to the thousands of nonprofits that are trying to do good in the world. What made him successful in his business could have helped so many more people. What a loss, and how sad.

He should have listened to my mother, who believed that giving is better than getting. It turns out, science agrees. A five-year study from the Science of Generosity Initiative at the University of Notre Dame surveyed 2,000 Americans and discovered that those who volunteered over five hours a month were more likely to rate themselves as "very happy." *Psychology Today* reports that the act of giving to others may increase the brain's levels of dopamine, lower blood pressure, combat loneliness and depression, and reduce chronic pain and stress. Each of these benefits boosts the individual's immune system, which in turn fights off disease and promotes a longer life. You don't need a lot of money—time can be just as valuable. Volunteering for a soup kitchen or collecting supplies for the homeless in your community are all ways to help others. These kinds of activities have an added bonus—they give you a sense of purpose and can motivate others to join you. I have always believed that spending money on others or giving your talent to causes that matter will put a bigger smile on your face than any Maserati or diamond earrings ever could. You can't take it with you, so what are you waiting for?

LATER = NEVER

For those of you who have made it this far, I have a dirty secret for you: I can't build anything. When I was at Handy Dan in the 1970s, I tried to do a plumbing job. I flooded the house, and the plumber made a deal with me: "If you promise to never touch another tool, I'll do any job for you for $50." I have kept that promise. I used to walk the stores, pick up a tool, and ask an associate to show me how to use it. I am not handy, and I'm not a do-it-yourselfer. I have never put up a fence, built a shed, or used a band saw. I decided early on that the only way I could really see how well our team worked was to stay willfully ignorant. This only worked if I knew less than they did. Then they had a chance to show me how well they could teach Home Depot customers. We were only as good as our worst teacher. I'm still stupid about tools, but the good news is that my grandson Joey can use every one in the store. Maybe there is hope for me yet.

I left Home Depot long ago, but I am as committed to the company as ever. I relish every triumph and was thrilled in October 2021 when *Forbes* magazine named Home Depot one of the World's Best Employers. We came in at #22 overall and #3 in the retail category for North and South America, right behind Costco Wholesale and IKEA. More than 700 companies were surveyed by 150,000 workers in 58 countries. In response to the news, then Home Depot chairman and CEO Craig Menear said, "Since the beginning, we've operated on the belief that if we take care of our associates, they'll take care of our customers, and the rest will take care of itself." I couldn't have said it better myself.

I don't have many regrets in my life, but one thing really bothers me. I was not around much for my children and grandchildren. While at Home Depot, I worked all the time. When I retired, I did the same thing with my philanthropy. Maybe it's because our family grew up poor, and I felt like I never had the luxury to slow down. Maybe it's because I've worked for so long that I can't imagine being without a job. Maybe it is because there is still so much to do.

I often have dinner with Joey, and one day we started

talking about this very subject. I tried to explain: "I have been a terrible grandfather. I missed so much of your childhood. I was always working. I know you have friends whose grandparents taught them to ride a bike, drive a tractor, or fly an airplane. I didn't have time for that." I think he understood that I have devoted my life to building something. I can't replace the time I've missed, but I can share what I've learned so they will be proud. That was one of the reasons I wanted to write this book.

My core lessons in business and life are easy to understand but sometimes hard to put into action:

First, you won't get anywhere if you don't believe that you can "do it yourself." No matter what task or problem, you need to be confident that you have the skills and determination to make things better. Some of those skills come from schooling, but you often learn the most from outside the classroom. On-the-job training and a thoughtful mentor can set you on the right track. It certainly worked for me.

My second lesson is that you don't have to do it alone. There are plenty of people who will help you if you let them. If you put in the hard work and embrace an entrepreneurial spirit, you are more likely to bring others along with you.

Third, you must have the burning desire to build something or fix something and be willing to commit the time, energy, and resources to dig in and make it work. There is no such thing as a part-time passion, just like there is no such thing as a part-time life. You have to be all in all the time.

Fourth, you have to take big risks that really fill a need or solve a problem and consider taking the biggest risks when you are young. You have the least to lose and time to rebound if necessary.

Fifth, when you fail—and you are going to fail plenty—you have to see it as the price you pay on your way to success. I have stumbled through my ninety plus years, but optimism fueled me.

The last lesson may be the most important one—you have to tell a compelling story about why your work, your project, your cause matters. Nobody will take you seriously if you can't articulate your value proposition in simple, understandable terms. Home Depot put everything you need under one roof, saved you money, and gave you the tools to do it yourself. Period. That was an easy sell, and everything we did to build the company was just a variation on that theme. So, take the time to really think about what matters and how you're going to achieve it. Burn that story into your psyche and be ready to sell your idea to anyone who will listen.

Embedded in each lesson is respect—for your ability to "do it yourself," for the people you work with and serve, for your passion, for the value of taking risks, for what you will learn from failure, and for the story you tell.

I'm a crummy but enthusiastic golfer. On a good day, I'm a twenty-handicapper or what they call a "bogey golfer." I'm lucky if I shoot in the nineties. The one round where I found myself walking to the eighteenth hole with a seventy-four on my card was interrupted by a freak lightning storm. I was playing in Atlanta at Peachtree Golf Club with Tom Cousins, and the golf pro had to actually come out in a cart to take my clubs from me so I wouldn't get killed. I framed the scorecard, but I'm still pretty steamed about it. Show me a successful retailer, and I'll show you a lousy golfer. I've always believed that your golf score increases in direct relation to your sales. I can live with being mediocre because I love being outside and enjoy the camaraderie with friends that is such an essential part of the game.

You are probably starting to ask yourself: "Bernie, what does golf have to do with respect?" In 1997, about seven weeks after he had prostate cancer surgery, Arnold Palmer joined me for a round of golf at Atlanta's East Lake Golf Club, where Bobby Jones learned to play. It was a beautiful day, and we decided to walk the course. I knew he wasn't feeling great, but every time he saw a member of the grounds crew working on a bunker or mowing, he walked over to shake hands and congratulate them on the course conditions. It slowed us down, but it was something to see. That man loved people, and his respect for their work was inspiring. Arnie reminded me that day that everybody is important, and if you denigrate waiters, salespeople, your employees, or the plumber who fixed your sink, it reveals a flaw in your character.

We probably won't ever meet, but I want you to know that you are never too young or too old to do something big. A quick Google search brings up dozens of stories of young entrepreneurs who know that starting young has some real advantages. You don't have a mortgage or spouse or three kids in college—which makes it easier to take a big chance. But youth can be an asset in another way—young entrepreneurs ask questions about things that everyone else assumes have been settled. They bring fresh eyes and new perspectives. I love their stories because they didn't wait for someone else to do the hard work—they did it themselves.

But there is also something to be said for the power of wisdom—you are never too old to be bold. Plenty of people did amazing things after the age of fifty—including me. Duncan Hines, who wrote food and hotel guides, licensed his name to be used on cake mixes at the age of seventy-three. Julia Child made her television debut at the age of fifty-one, and Charles Darwin wrote *On the Or-*

igin of Species at the age of fifty, just about the age I was when we started Home Depot.

I love the story of Harland Sanders, who founded Kentucky Fried Chicken. The Colonel had a pretty rocky road on his way to success. He was born in 1890, his father died when he was very young, and he took over caring for his younger siblings. He started working as a farmer at the age of ten and got fired from a dozen jobs, including streetcar conductor, railroad fireman, and tire and insurance salesman. He ran a gas station and restaurant that catered to tired travelers, but in the 1950s, the highway junction in front of his place was moved, so he auctioned off the site. Without any income, he started traveling around the nation looking for potential restaurants and offering them his now-famous recipe in return for four cents on every chicken sold. By 1964, at the age of seventy-four and with more than six hundred franchised outlets, he sold his interest in the company for $2 million and stayed the iconic face of the company until his death in 1980.

THE ONE THING THAT THESE ENTREPRENEURS, YOUNG and old, have in common is that they live in a country that makes all this possible. The American Dream is not dead.

It may sound a little corny, but I still believe that we live in the land of opportunity. Where else could a poor kid from Newark build the largest home improvement retail company in the world, create an entire industry, and give away $2 billion? I am so fortunate that my parents came to a country that cherishes free enterprise and allows it to flourish. I believe that if you work hard enough you can make a difference. Success means different things to different people—but for me it boils down to one simple question: Did I make anybody's life better? I'd like to think that this book answers that.

I hope my story brings with it some lessons that will motivate you to do something you really care about. When should you try to start a new business or help a worthy cause? Now. It doesn't matter if you are eighteen or eighty. When are you too old to do something important? Never. Just because you have retired and have grandchildren doesn't mean your life is over. I didn't get my big break until I was almost fifty. So get out there and do some good because later equals never. I just wish I had another lifetime to see you do it.

ACKNOWLEDGMENTS

FROM BERNIE

I want to begin by thanking all the associates and customers at Home Depot. They helped build a great company and have created the wealth that allows us to participate in all this charitable work. I'm not exaggerating when I say that this would not have been possible without their hard work, dedication, and loyalty. I also want to thank the hundreds of universities, organizations, and nonprofits around the nation and in Israel that are trying to repair the world. It is our pleasure to support and partner with them at the Marcus Foundation and to see the work they do in literally hundreds of arenas.

I have been so lucky to have great partners and colleagues throughout my life, and I owe a special thanks to my parents, siblings, family, Herbie Hubschman, Sam

Walton, Arthur Blank, Ken Langone, Rip Fleming, Ron Brill, Pat Farrah, Frank Blake, George Shultz, Gary Sinise, Pitbull, Rick Slagle, Steven Hantler, Dr. Jeffrey Koplan, and all the people that helped me along the way. I could probably list a thousand more names, but the publisher won't let me. Know that you are in my heart, and that I am overwhelmed by gratitude for everything you have done with and for me.

This book was Jay Kaiman's idea, and he stayed with us every step of the way. Jay probably knows me better than anyone, and I am so appreciative of his vision for this project and helping to bring it to fruition. Leslie King was instrumental with scheduling our meetings and a hundred other things. Thanks to the whole team at the Marcus Foundation, including Renay Blumenthal, Donna Englander Fleishman, Gretchen Seyba, Dr. Jonathan Simons, Dr. Fred Sanfilippo, and Marcus Ruzek, who helped us with various parts of the story. Their contributions have been invaluable.

Special thanks to my family, especially my son Fred, who took it upon himself to make sure that we got the book we wanted. He was a critical part of the process and shepherded the book between Atlanta and Florida, sitting for hours as we worked on draft after draft. He is a true mensch. My son Michael helped us identify family photographs along with Rachel Slomovitz. The team at Home

Depot, notably Jennifer Wyatt, the corporate archivist, was a terrific fact checker and found some great photographs from our early days. Craig Menear, chairman of the board, and Ted Decker, CEO and president of Home Depot, were a big help, and I appreciate all of their support. I also wanted to thank my dear friends Lynne and Howard Halpern, and Mike and Andrea Leven.

A very special thanks to our agent, Esmond Harmsworth at Aevitas, who shared our vision from the outset. He guided us through the whole project and deserves a heartfelt thanks. The staff at William Morrow has been terrific to work with, and special thanks to Nick Amphlett, Kayleigh George, and their whole team.

This project started as a collaboration, and I am so grateful that I had a chance to write it with Dr. Catherine Lewis. She is a respected historian and university administrator at Kennesaw State University, who had written fourteen other books, so she knew what she was doing. We talked for hours, had a lot of laughs, and she worked tirelessly to bring my story forth. The highest compliment that I can pay her is that she found my voice. I am eternally grateful to her for that.

Finally, I want to thank my wife, Billi, who had been with me on this journey for a million years. She is my best friend and the love of my life, and after nearly 50 years together, I can still say that I married up.

ACKNOWLEDGMENTS

FROM CATHERINE

Writing a book together is no easy feat; your relationship has to be built on mutual respect and admiration. I'm lucky to say that Bernie and I had both. I cannot think of a better storyteller or partner, and it has been my pleasure to bring *Kick Up Some Dust* to publication. His story is the very embodiment of the American dream—filled with hardship, grit, generosity, and determination. Anyone who wants to make it big would be wise to read this book.

I had so much help along the way, and Bernie has already thanked so many of the people that assisted us. Jay Kaiman deserves special recognition. He carried this book from beginning to end, and our success is due to his unwavering commitment. As always, I have personal debts to pay—to my colleagues in the Kennesaw State University Department of Museums, Archives and Rare Books who are great sounding boards; to Jennifer Wyatt at Home Depot, who is a terrific archivist at Home Depot and sounding board; to Karen Grinzaid at JScreen; to my sister Shelley Andrew for her enduring support; and to my husband, John Companiotte, an accomplished author in his own right. A sweet thank you to my daughter, Emma, who loved hearing Bernie's stories and patiently tolerated her mother's many late nights. A final thank you to my father, Dr. J. Richard Lewis, who passed in No-

ACKNOWLEDGMENTS

vember of 2020, while we were working on the book. He was a scholar and accomplished author, and we shared a lifelong love of literature and history. I read him drafts of the manuscript up to the day he died. He made me the writer, historian, and person that I am, and that is a debt I can relish but never truly repay.

ABOUT THE AUTHORS

Bernie Marcus co-founded Home Depot, the world's largest home improvement retailer, and served as its inaugural CEO and as its chairman until his retirement in 2002. Over the last several decades, he has redirected his entrepreneurial spirit toward hundreds of charitable endeavors to solve big problems. He has given away more than $2 billion and is a signatory of the Giving Pledge.

Dr. Catherine Lewis is assistant vice president of Museums, Archives and Rare Books; director of the Museum of History and Holocaust Education; and professor of history at Kennesaw State University. She is the author, co-author, or co-editor of fifteen books.